CARLO'S ICE CREAM AND TEA ROOMS

GENERATIONAL ORAL HISTORY OF AN ANGLO-ITALIAN FAMILY

From. Sue + Reg for 81st. Birthday

CHRISTINE P. TANNER

This work has been recorded, transcribed, edited, researched and written by
Christine P Tanner MSc DipSW, Oral Historian

I am a member of the Oral History Society and follow their Code of Ethics

**Carlo and Anthony Donnarumma and Stella Wilde, nee Donnarumma,
relate their memories in their own words**

ISBN 978-0-9569776-0-1

Published by

CPT Oral History
cptoralhistory@gmail.com

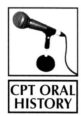

cptoralhistory.blogspot.com

"Carlo's Ice Cream Parlour and Tea Rooms -
Generational Oral History of an Anglo-Italian Family".

Cover and Book Designed and Typeset by Matt Swann
21stbookdesign.blogspot.com

Printed by Hobbs the Printers Ltd, Totton, Hants.

Profits from this publication will be donated to
Romsey and Wellow Group of Friends of
Cancer Research UK (Registered Charity 1089464)

In memory of my parents
John Frederick May and Gwendoline Eva May

This book is dedicated to my sons
Julian and Alastair

CONTENTS

ACKNOWLEDGMENTS

First and foremost, I should like to thank Anthony Donnarumma (Tony) and his wife, Barbara, owners of Carlo's Ice Cream Parlour and Tea Rooms, West Wellow, near Romsey, Hampshire, England, for their friendship and support in the writing of this book. Without my recording of Tony's life in 2008 this book containing generational oral history would not have been written. I should also like to thank them for their company on our short sojourn to Minori on the Amalfi Coast.

Equally important of course, was the involvement of Tony's father, Carlo Donnarumma, whom I interviewed and recorded in 1985. Carlo's wife, Thora, was also supportive throughout that time. Sadly, both Carlo and Thora are now deceased.

Thanks are also due to Tony and Barbara's children, Beverley Davies and Anton Donnarumma, and to the permanent staff of the tea rooms, Wayne Shaw and Sadie Bevan, led by Beverley Davies. I also thank two grand-sons, Jamie Donnarumma and Christopher Davies. Christopher is a budding top Chef who has prepared several wonderful meals for us all.

I should like to thank Stella Wilde (nee Donnarumma, Nicolo's daughter) who in 2010 kindly allowed me to record her memories. Her daughter, Linda Cadier (nee Wilde) was of great help to me. My gratitude is due to Stella's nephew, Brian Donnarumma, who gave me a handed-down family tree dating back to 1814 which was researched and compiled by his Uncle Raymond and Julie (Angela Maria) Donnarumma (both now deceased) in Minori in the early 1990's. I trust my own research and addition is without error.

Other members of the Donnarumma family - my gratitude is due to Elise Edwards (nee Donnarumma, daughter of Francesco 'Babe'), Eleanora (Yana) Peden (deceased) nee Donnarumma whom I met in 1985 when she came into Tudor House Museum with a collection of old photographs. She kindly allowed us to make negatives of these. A special thank you to John Richardson, Clotilda's (Goodie's) son, from Scotland.

In Minori I was treated with great kindness by Signora Maria Esposito, her daughter and son-in-law, Trofimena and Ciro Apicella, and her grand-daughter, Rosa Apicella from Milan who helped with some interpretation. Grazie mille. Grazie also to Signore Antonio Pappalardo, L'Ufficiale dello Stato Civile.

I should also like to thank the following:

Jeanne Simkin for proof-reading the manuscript.

Kay Lorenzato of the Anglo-Italian Family History Society www.anglo-italianfhs.org.uk and for her assistance at the Archives of St Peter's Italian Church, Holborn, London.

Tudor Allen and the staff of Camden Local Studies and Archives Centre, London.

Joanne Smith and Susan Hill at Southampton City Archives.

Martin Windess, Volunteer, Southampton City Archives.

David Hollingworth and Vicky Green, Local Studies and Maritime Collections, Central Library, Southampton.

Padmini Broomfield, Lead Outreach Projects Officer, (also Oral Historian), Arts and Heritage, Southampton City Council.

Sheila Jemima, Oral Historian and retired Manager, Southampton City Council's Oral History Unit (now closed).

Ernest Spacagna and his son, Mario Spacagna.

Jez Gale of the Archives of the Southern Daily Echo, Southampton.

Janet Tudball of The Romsey Advertiser. The staff at Romsey and Salisbury Libraries.

Phoebe Merrick, Lower Test Valley Archaeological Study Group LTVAS Romsey Town Hall.

Olwen Rowlands for teaching and translation of Italian language.

Christopher Squires, "Save Those Memories", Swindon, Wiltshire.

Volunteers, Diane Blackburn, Pam Cotton and Jill Green and Helpers, Romsey and Wellow Group of Friends of Cancer Research UK.

Michael Sleigh, Wellow History Society. With thanks for supporting Cancer Research UK

Matt Swann, Book Designer - 21stBookDesign. A special thank you for your great patience.

Hobbs the Printers Ltd. Totton, Hampshire. Thank you for supporting Cancer Research UK

Pamela Donnaruma, Publisher and Editor, The Boston Post Gazette, Boston, USA.

Last but not least, my great appreciation is to my husband, Andrew who gave many hours of his time assisting me in the operation of scanners, computers and cameras.

FOREWORD

Twenty-six years ago, in January 1985, I had the privilege of recording some memories of Mr Carlo Donnarumma for an Oral History project about the Chapel and Northam communities of Southampton before the lst and 2nd World Wars.

For five years from 1984 I was a member of the Oral History team then based at Tudor House Museum, Southampton. In 1985 at the close of the Chapel and Northam year-long project our team at the time, consisting of myself, Sheila Jemima, Tim Caves, Sharon Taffe, Photograper Dave Roberts, and led by Carl Major - with the very patient and accurate visually-impaired audio-typist, Sue Dixon - produced a public Exhibition staged within Tudor House.

On the opening day interviewees brought their families and friends, some later revisiting several times. Many had never before stepped inside a museum. Consequently, to see and hear their family name, their photographs displayed and their stories told was a proud moment - as they related to me afterwards.

Needless to say, home-made ice cream was provided for the event by the generosity of Carlo Donnarumma and this was complemented by the Oral History Team's 'pick-your- own' strawberries. The sun shone down on us in the Tudor House garden. It was a day to remember.

The concept of an Oral History Archive for Southampton Museums was first introduced in 1983 by the then Museums Education and Outreach Officer, Dr Sian Jones. The first projects were entitled "Women's' War Work - 1st World War" and "Working the Port" - Southampton Docks before 1940. At the same time the Maritime Historian, Alastair Forsythe (prematurely deceased) produced an Exhibition entitled "Art on the Liners". Alastair was to become an important fount of knowledge to us all since he knew all there was to know about cruise ships from their inception. Alastair was also my co-interviewer for the life-recording of Commodore Geoffrey Marr DSC RD RNR, Commodore of the Cunard Fleet 1966-1971.

These projects were followed in 1984 by "Chapel and Northam - Southampton's Dockland Communities 1900-1945" plus an Afro-Caribbean project - recordings by Dawn McCollin, later Haynes (prematurely deceased) and researched by Ron Belgrave. In addition, we staged an Exhibition of family photographs we had collected called "Peoples' Pictures". The photographs were enlarged and mounted and then hung in the Southampton Art Gallery. The Opening was enhanced by swing and dance-band music by John May's Band (my father, now deceased). Those hallowed galleries had seen nothing like it!

By 1986 the project "Woolston Before the Bridge" had begun, together with projects of a maritime theme. Many recordings were extensive, full life-histories. We made excerpt tapes for educational, presentation, publication or exhibition use. Our outreach work included taking artefacts, image presentations and the oral history extracts into schools, old people's homes and to local history groups.

From late 1989 until my retirement I pursued another career. Since my retirement I have been variously involved in voluntary Oral History work for the University of Southampton's Basque children's project "Los Ninos" of the Spanish Civil War and with Southampton City Council's Oral History Unit (now sadly just recently closed). I was also involved with teaching Oral History to Salisbury U3A groups, and with writing articles about my own family members whom I had recorded years ago.

Listening to my old recordings gave me an interest to explore 'Generational' Oral History and to 're-visit' some of the interviewees or their next 'generation' to discover what had happened to them and their descendants. This is what led me to eventually record the memories of Carlo Donnarumma's son, Anthony Carlo Donnarumma (Tony) in 2008 and his older cousin, Stella Wilde, nee Donnarumma, in 2010. Sadly, Carlo had died in 1990. I have now met many members of the Donnarumma family descendents, including some in Minori, Southern Italy. There is, of course, still much that could be researched, in both England and Minori. It is of interest that the first British generation of Donnarumma offspring, who are now all deceased, integrated and assimilated the English culture so readily whilst, of course, still retaining Neapolitan mores. The fascinating journey of producing this book has been a pleasure and privilege.

It is my observation, and those of others, that every oral history recording is subjective and that no two people, even if related, experience the same situation exactly alike. Whilst there were memories and many facts I discovered which it feels prudent to exclude from this book, I have endeavoured to represent the different views and stories of the members of the Donnarumma family, together with my own research. Essentially however, their stories are in their own words and I have tried to link photographs to those words.

Of the three Donnarumma brothers who came to England in 1894 or before, Nicolo, Carlo and Achille, there are many grandchildren and great-grandchildren living in Great Britain today. Many of these have become professionally skilled and successful. This story continues following the line of Achille, Achille's second child, Carlo, and Carlo's son, Anthony Carlo.

The leitmotif of the book is the continuing successful entrepreneurial factory-owning, shop keeping, catering and ice cream making threads that run through the family from 1814 to the present day. This has often been against all odds - more recently from Anthony Donnarumma's grandfather Achille, his own father Carlo, to himself, to his daughter Beverley Davies, and to his grandson, Christopher Davies. Christopher has trained under Marcus Wareing and been employed in a Gordon Ramsay company. He is currently developing his career as a Chef at a five-star hotel.

This is a true story of impoverishment to accomplishment by poor Southern Italian immigrants who came to England newly married in 1905 - Achille Donnarumma and Trofimena Proto. As I have discovered, there were in the past members of the Donnarumma family in Minori who were not poor and would have been prominent pillars of society in their day, namely a Priest, an Industrialist and possibly others.

Christine P Tanner

Oral Historian

Summer 2011

Carlo Donnarumma's Oral History interview can be heard at Southampton City Archives. The interviews of Anthony Carlo Donnarumma and Stella Wilde (nee Donnarumma) will be deposited with the Southampton City Archives in due course.

MAP OF ITALY

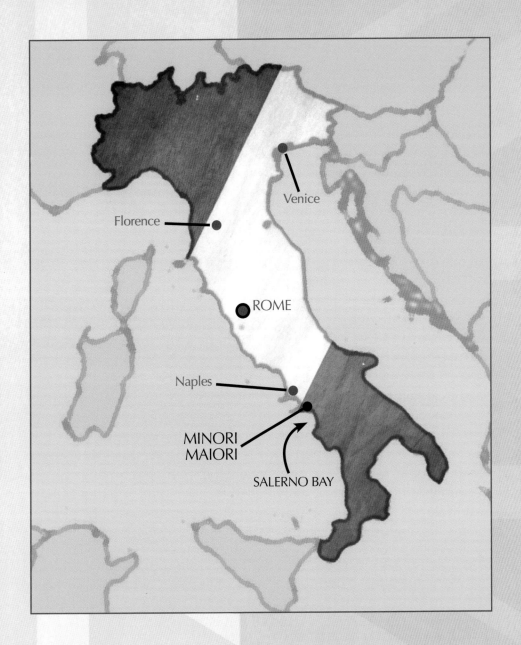

Venice

Florence

ROME

Naples

MINORI
MAIORI

SALERNO BAY

CHAPTER 1
The Italian Heritage

The story begins in the 19th century in the small town of Minori on the Amalfi Coast in the province of Salerno within the Campania Region of south-west Italy. Its ancient Latin name was Rheginna Minor. It is the minor town of its close neighbour, Rheginna Maiori (major) which is famous for the longest unbroken stretch of beach along the Amalfi Coast and in ancient times was an important harbour.

At one time Minori was more important than Maiori due to its industries of paper-making, pasta-making, hide tanning and exporting of citrus fruits. It was also an arsenal of the Maritime Republic of Amalfi and therefore a military force on a par with the powerful town of Amalfi. In 1597 a violent storm destroyed the main square and the town walls of Minori. Periodic floods have also ravaged Maiori, the most recent being in 1910 and 1954. In 1954 Maiori's Medieval heart was destroyed and many of its historical buildings were swept away. Both Minori and Maiori are crossed by two rivers with different courses. These rivers can be almost dry all year but can change to a torrential flow in rainy periods. At these times they can be subject to flooding due to deforestation which has exposed the hinterland to erosion. Between the towns and hills of Minori and Maiori is the Valley of Tramonti. The term "transmonti" simply means 'through the mountains'.

The town of Minori rises from the beach, along the valley and up the steep hillsides. There are a host of terraces which have been laboriously dug out of these steep slopes for cultivation. Even today there is just a population of around three thousand.

Minori at the turn of the Twentieth Century. Collection of Maurizio Apicella.

Villa Romana - (Villa Marittima) Minori

Minori was a favourite resort of the patricians of ancient Rome and in the Julio-Claudian period (63BC to 14AD) the Romans built an important villa here, the ruins of which are open today for public viewing. The villa was discovered in 1932 but not excavated until the 1950's. It stood in the pleasant valley surrounded by the steep hills with the open sea to the south. Today its surroundings are part of the town. It was built on two floors around a vast court-yard, graced by a pool and surrounded by a portico. Its walls were richly decorated with frescoes, mosaics and stucco work. The private thermal baths have been perfectly preserved.

The author at Villa Romana Collonade, Minori, 2011.

Churches of Minori

Minori's important Basilica was built on the original site of an ancient Roman church. Santa Trofimena is the venerated Roman Catholic canonised female saint of this Basilica. Her relics are reputed to be contained within the alabaster urn on the main alter and there are solemn celebrations in honour of her throughout the year, the most important being in July.

Basilica St Trophimena, Minori, 2011.

San Giovanni Picolo was built in the 15th century. It is situated on the steps to the west of the town and is recognizable by its oval window, small arch and bells above the door. The 10th century church of Santa Lucia is attached to the Benedictine monastery and is near the Alla Fiumara district. Destruction caused by war has left only a part of this church in existence.

At the height of the town, called Villamena, are the churches of Santa Maria delle Grazie and San Gennaro e Giuliano. The chapel of Annunziata was dismantled in 1950 due to its damaged structure and only the late 13th century bell-tower remains.

Hand-Made Paper Manufacturing

As far back as the 6th century AD the Amalfi Republic was a sea power with a wide network of sea routes and an important trading influence in the Mediterranean between 839 AD until around 1200 AD. The Amalfi merchants were using gold coins to purchase land in the 9th century AD whilst most of Italy still worked on a barter system. They bought silks from the Byzantine Empire and re-sold it to the West. They also traded in salt from Sardinia and timber and grain from neighbouring countries.

There was a high demand for paper to document these many transactions between merchants. After discovering the closely guarded secret of paper manufacture from the Arabs, who learnt it from the Egyptians, the region became one of the centres for this craft. This industry eventually dwindled, though with the economic improvement in the 16th and 17th centuries, it was revived and at least sixteen paper mills were established. In Amalfi today there is a paper-making museum (Museo della Carta) dedicated to the making of the famous Amalfi hand-made paper. In the present day there are still producers of this hand-made paper in Amalfi and until recently, in Minori. Traditional methods are used to make the paper to reproduce old prints, wood engravings, writing paper and to print valuable artistic editions of books. Some also specialise in producing elegant wedding stationery.

Pasta Making

Although the oldest noodle-like foods have been found in China, they were made from millet so the origins of pasta continues to evoke speculation. The familiar legend of Marco Polo (1254-1324 AD) importing pasta into Italy from China might well be a myth since durum wheat, from which Italian pasta is traditionally made, was not known in China until more recent years. It would appear that durum wheat was introduced into Italy by the Arabs during their conquest of Sicily in the late 7th century.

Types of pasta, such as lasagne, had been known in ancient Greece and Rome. Vermicelli was known in Medieval Italy. By the late 16th century, with increasing world trading, there became a need for a type of food which could easily be stored on board ship for long voyages. Sailors from Amalfi on their frequent voyages to Sicily, brought the Sicilian art of drying pasta back home.

More recently, the inhabitants of Amalfi were fishermen, lemon and olive growers, producers of olive oil, grapes and wine, and farmers of small plots producing vegetables and fruit. They were also manufacturers of traditional pasta. Indeed, the 'paste della Costa' was well-known in the 18th and 19th centuries in southern Italy. During the 18th century a considerable percentage of the Amalfi population worked in pasta factories. As far back as the 16th century they were producing macaroni, vermicelli, tagliatelli, gniochelli, fusilli and later spaghetti. The generalised word 'pasta' was not adopted until recent times, the word 'macaroni' being its popular description.

Ceramics and Mosaics - Terrazzo

Due to the local earth being rich in clay and volcanic content, Minori and the areas of the Amalfi Coast have produced ceramics, beautiful floor and wall tiles and mosaics for thousands of years. Today these creational arts still survive.

Minori ceramics of the present day, 2011.

A Brief History of Ice Cream Making

In ancient times the people of the Persian Empire would pour grape juice over snow in a bowl and eat this as a treat similar to ice cream. They mastered the technique of storing ice inside naturally cooled areas known as Yakhchals (meaning ice pit). The Roman Emperor Nero (37-68 AD) who ruled between 54-68 AD had snow brought in from the mountains and combined it with fruit toppings.

The Arabs were the first to use milk or cream as a major ingredient of this dessert and to sweeten it with sugar rather than fruit juices. They were doing this as early as the 10th century. However, it would appear that the Chinese invented a device to make sorbet and ice desserts by coating snow and saltpetre over the exterior of vessels containing syrup. It has been claimed that in the Yuan Dynasty, Kublai Khan (1215-1294) enjoyed ice cream and kept it a royal secret until Marco Polo (1254-1324) visited China and eventually, after staying twenty-four years there, took the technique of ice cream making back to Italy. However, the Italians have arguably been making something resembling ice cream before Marco Polo returned to Italy.

When the Italian duchess Catherine de Medici married the Duc d'Orleans in 1533 she is said to have brought with her Italian chefs who introduced ice cream into France. By the 19th century recipes had reached throughout Europe and eventually to the United States and the rest of the world.

Ice cream remained an expensive and rare treat and mostly available to wealthy people with access to an ice house. Ice cream was first made available to the general public in England by the Italian-Swiss entrepreneur, Carlo Gatti (1817-1878) when he opened an ice cream stall outside Charing Cross Station in 1851. Gatti also opened a stand in Hungerford Market near Charing Cross, to sell pastries and ice cream. A portion of ice cream was sold for one penny served in a shell and later in a small glass container called the 'penny lick'.

The 'penny lick' was banned in London in 1899 due to concerns about the spread of disease as the glasses were often inadequately washed between customers. Following that waxed paper, the ice biscuit, the waffle and ice cream cones were developed, which saved the street ice cream industry. Italian ice cream vendors in Britain in the late 19th and the early 20th centuries famously became known as 'hokey pokey' men from their street cries of "Ecco un poco" meaning 'here is a little piece', or 'here is a little price'.

'Penny Lick' ice cream glasses, 1890's.

Ice cream was made in the domestic setting by the boiling of milk which was then left to cool overnight. Zinc drums were placed inside wooden barrels and the space between the two was packed with crushed ice and salt, forming a cold brine. The milk was flavoured and then poured into the inner zinc drums which were then hand-turned until the contents eventually froze and ice cream was formed. The process of hand-cranking was labour-intensive. Later, the invention of the mechanical process was to relieve this. Ice cream makers developed their own original recipes using fresh milk, sugar, butter, cream or eggs and various flavourings. These original recipes were later handed down within families and some of them survive and are still used today.

In Britain the hand-made ice cream was sold from barrels on street corners, from stands, stalls and from horse-drawn or hand-pushed carts and barrows. The carts and barrows were hand-made and decorated individually, many bearing the owner's name. Often the seller would be accompanied by an organ grinder, his music announcing their arrival – much like the later times of the tricycle and bell and the present time of the ice cream van with jingle music.

Why Did Italians Leave Italy in the 19th and 20th Centuries?

From around 500 AD the peninsula of Italy consisted of several independent regions. They were variously fought over and ruled by Germans, Byzantines, French, Spanish, Prussians and Austrians until the 1850s. Following the defeat of the Austrians, 'Risorgimento' (Resurgence) slowly evolved. This was the political and social process that unified the different states and kingdoms of the Italian peninsular into the single nation of Italy. The three founding fathers of this process were Giuseppe Mazzini, Count Camillo Cavour and Guiseppe Garibaldi. The kingdom of Italy was proclaimed in Turin in 1861 with Vittorio Emmanuele II as King. Italy was to be involved in many more wars before it became a Republic in 1946.

By the beginning of the 19th century rural Italy had experienced major changes, partly the result of a vastly increasing population and the twenty-year occupation of Napoleon's armies who had lived off the land. Common and church lands were redistributed to Italian aristocracy who were supporters of Napoleon and small kingdoms evolved. This led to a dispossession of small farmers because they had to pay taxes they could not afford. Subsequently, seasonal migration began, predominantly from northern and mid Italy, mostly to Austria, Switzerland, France and Germany, with small numbers ending up in Britain.

Conditions in Italy steadily deteriorated further throughout the nineteenth century, created by wars, deforestation, industrialisation, taxes and diseases such as cholera and malaria. Eventually, the economy collapsed, causing famines and the mass migrations. Between 1862 and 1891 over four million people left Italy and from 1900-1910 more than another million were lost to Italy. From 1889 to 1905 immigrants to Britain were predominantly from southern Italy which was an even poorer area in a land that definitely had, and still has today, a north/south divide.

The majority headed for USA, though some emigrated to other European countries or to Argentina, Brazil and to Great Britain, where they made a living as organ grinders, knife sharpeners, ice cream makers, chestnut vendors, plaster figure makers, confectioners, and keepers of small provision shops and cafes. Others worked as seamen and in jobs that maintained the shipping industry.

Many in the Italian Merchant Navy were seduced by the higher wages in the British Merchant Navy. Often their work was seasonal and they returned to Italy periodically. They contributed to the Italian economy by taking or sending money to their poorer relatives at home in Italy.

Minori waterfront with fountain. Late 19th century. Collection of Gennaro Apicella.

There also emerged in Britain what became known as the 'Padrone' system where more established male emigrants acted as an 'agent' or 'master' using the village or family connections in Italy to recruit workers, in the earlier times mostly very young male adults or boys as young as ten or eleven, to bring to England. The Padrone 'master' would offer a 'contract' to the mother to take her son, pay for his passage or walk with him and others across France. Once in England they would bear the responsibility for their lodgings and food and they would work for the two to three year 'contract' usually without pay, sometimes with a promise of a bonus at the end of their time which they did not always receive.

Some Padrone 'masters' exploited their Padroni workers, gave them little food, treated them cruelly and kept them in overcrowded, squalid accommodation, from which they could not escape due to lack of money, their passports, if any, held by their 'master', and their inability to speak English. Often 'masters' worked in pairs, one in England whilst the other was recruiting in Italy. Accommodation could be described as 'depots' - mostly in London but with several independent centres in different cities or port towns so that the Padroni 'servant' could be distributed where needed. Some Padrone 'masters' were honourable and their 'servants' were eventually able to return to Italy or establish themselves independently in Britain.

The Padrone system continued in Britain until the late 1920s though after the introduction of the Aliens Act of 1905 which removed itinerancy, independent family-based businesses began to materialise and the older custom of Padrone controlling large numbers of people died out. The family-base brought about changes and girls were brought in from Italy to work as domestic servants and nannies to children of the Padrone. Developments from this were the successful lives of these Padroni, sometimes with the assistance of their Padrone 'masters'.

The immigrants to London became the founders of the 'Italian Colony' which came to be known as "Little Italy" in Clerkenwell and Holborn. This 'colony' emerged by the process of 'chain migration' whereby a 'pioneer' (the most notable becoming a Padrone master) from a certain area or village in Italy would travel to Britain, establish himself and thereafter bring in his family, his relatives and perhaps fellow villagers known as 'paesani'. This has resulted in many villages or areas of Italy having affiliation with specific towns and cities throughout the world.

Minori waterfront looking west. Late 19th century. Collection of Gennaro Apicella.

CHAPTER 2
The Donnarumma Family

Chapter 1 was the background heritage to the life of the young Achille Donnarumma, born in Minori on 1st March 1880. Achille's parents were Domenico Donnarumma (born 1848) and Mariantonia Clotilde (nee Lembo) who were married in Minori on 7th September 1873. They had three sons, Nicolo born 1877, Carlo born 1878 and Achille born 1880. It is not known if there were more children but these three sons were destined to spend their adult lives in England.

Achille's grandfather, Nicolo (born 1817) who was the Organist in the Basilica of St Trofimena, married Marianna (nee Fago) in 1845 and they had eight children. Achille's father, Domenico, followed in his own father's footsteps to become the Church Organist of the Basilica.

Family records have been traced further back, with the knowledge that Achille's great-grandfather was a Domenico Donnarumma (born 1792) who had married Trofimena (nee Ruocco, 1797-1894) in 1814 and had nine children. Their eldest child Reginaldo Donnarumma (born 1815) became an 'Industrialist' who owned a factory in Minori, possibly a ceramics, pasta or paper-making factory. Reginaldo married Madalena Landi and one of their children, a Carlo Matteo Donnarumma, born on 16th January 1849 was to become the High Priest of the Cathedral of St Trofimena in Minori. He died on 24th January 1922 aged 73. His ornate tomb, notably not shared, is in the cemetery at Minori.

Tomb of Can.D. Carlo Matteo Donnarumma, High Priest of the Basilica of St Trofimena, Minori cemetery. 'Can.D' can be interpreted as 'Diocesian Candidate or Diocesian Canon, meaning the Priest appointed to the Diocese by the Bishop.

The first Donnarumma documented to have come to England was Achille's uncle Francesco (born 1862) who, on the 1891 UK Census is recorded as being 29 years, single, living in lodgings in Clerkenwell and with an occupation of Ice Cream Hawker and Ice Maker. Francesco Donnarumma was married aged 35 years in St Peter's Italian Church, Holborn in 1897 to Stella Napolitana aged 24 years. Francesco was literate though his wife was not. On his marriage certificate the profession of his father, Nicolo (Achille's grandfather, born 1817) is recorded as 'Organist'.

Another Donnarumma immigrant to England, probably a cousin of Achille's, named Antonio was married in 1900 aged 25 years, at St Peter's Italian Church, Holborn to Carolina Mansi, aged 24 years. Neither was literate. Antonio's profession is stated as 'Ice Cream Vendor'. His father's name was Pietro Donnarumma, a farmer.

Of the three Donnarumma brothers who came to England; Nicolo stayed in London whilst Carlo and Achille eventually settled in Southampton. When Nicolo married aged 28 years to Rose McBride aged 28 years at St Peter's Italian Church, Holborn in 1905, his profession was stated as being an Artist's Model living in Clerkenwell and that his father Domenico (born 1848) had the profession of 'Organist'. The Italian Neapolitan classical looks made them sought-after as models for leading British artists of the day. Indeed, Nicolo is listed as having modelled six times in 1906 and once in 1907 (draped for painting students) and paid seven shillings each sitting - all sittings were at the prestigious Royal Academy of Arts. It is believed that Nicolo and his wife, Rose, eventually ran a fruiterer shop in London and imported Italian produce. They had many children.

A further corroborating fact in relation to the church organist tradition is on the marriage certificate of Carlo, aged 32 years, to Amelia Norah Ryan aged 17 years, in 1910 at St Joseph's Roman Catholic Chapel in Southampton, where it is stated that his father, Domenico (born 1848) was a 'Church Organist.'

Some branches of the Donnarumma family from southern Italy emigrated to the USA and other parts of the world. The spelling of the surname has been variously altered both here and abroad.

Minori and Trofimena are important names in the Donnarumma family history. Achille, married Trofimena Proto in Minori on 20th July 1905. At the time Achille was literate though his wife was not. Trofimena was born in Minori on 11th March 1879. Their communion was to result in several generations of descendants, mostly still living in Southampton, England. From the foregoing it can be seen that ice cream making and vending was one of the professions of the Donnarumma family in England from at least 1891 and possibly before. Church music, pasta-making, accordion and piano music, shop-keeping, cooking and catering were also in their blood.

Minori waterfront, fishing boat. Late 19th century. Collection Gennaro Apicella.

There is an early Donnarumma Family Tree in Appendix I on page 118

CHAPTER 3
A New Life in England

The family believe that Achille Donnarumma first arrived in England in 1894 when he was just 14 years old. They also believe he travelled to New York though I can find no record of this in the Ellis Island website. The earliest recorded presence of Achille Donnarumma in Britain is on the 1901 England Census. He was aged 22 years and living almost within the "Little Italy" area of Clerkenwell in St Botolph-within-Bishopsgate, London. From the Census form we know that Achille was one of six, single Italian male 'servants' lodging with an Italian, his wife and family. The tenant was most probably the Padrone 'master' to the six 'lodgers'. They all hailed from the same part of southern Italy as the 'master'. They worked as Bread-makers and Confectioners and were possibly also making and selling ice cream.

Achille and his older brother, Carlo, as aforementioned, ultimately settled in Southampton. Working conditions and wages in many trades in Southampton and throughout Britain in 1900 were deplorable. However, the Port of Southampton was developing and expanding to accommodate large ships which brought commerce and passenger traffic. Such a port attracted immigrants with an entrepreneurial spirit.

According to Kelly's Directory of Southampton and Neighbourhood 1904, a Mr George Carlow (Carlo Donnarumma) lived at 3 Lime Street and by 1905 at a lodging house at 38 King Street. Records tell us that Carlo called himself Mr Edward Carlo though by 1914 he had changed this to Mr George Carlo. By 1908/9 Mr Edward Carlo was living at 18 East Street where he ran a shop selling fruit and flowers and lived above the shop, though he possibly rented a lodging house for his Padroni workers. At the time East Street was one of the main shopping streets of old Southampton - a prestigious location. He was to remain there until his untimely death in 1923 when he was just 45 years old. He left a wife and six children.

His death certificate describes his occupations as 'Fruiterer and Master'. It is believed his wife Nora, then known as 'Mrs Carlo' ran the shop with her new husband, Nicolo Donnarumma (Achille's eldest son), for just two or three more years with the help of an English shop manager named Charlie John Sutton.

By 1905 Achille had returned to Minori where he married Trofimena Proto. Her surname 'Proto' appears as 'Prota' on several of her children's British birth certificates and their surname is variously spelt. A year later Achille and Trofimena were living at the lodging house, 38 King Street and it was here that their first child, Nicolo, was born in 1906. In 1908 at the lodging house, 19 King Street, their second child (the subject of the title of this book) was born and named Carlo, after his uncle. Thereafter, Achille and Trofimena had five more children, Domenico, born 1909, Eleanora (known as Yana) born 1911, Clotilda (known as Goodie) born 1912, Amalia (known as Emily) born 1913. Finally, Francesco was born in late 1915 at 14 Canal Walk. He was often known throughout his life as 'Babe'.

King Street, Southampton c1910 The Fella family and/or the Pagliare and Donnarumma families (exact details unknown). Courtesy of Local Studies and Maritime Collections, Central Library, Southampton.

The three Donnarumma brothers, Achille, Carlo and Nicolo all appear on the 1911 Census of England. Nicolo was living at 151 Offord Road, Islington, London, Carlo was living at 18 East Street, Southampton and Achille was living at 19 King Street, Southampton. Nicolo was a Fruiterer and Greengrocer, Carlo was a Fruiterer and Flower-seller, whilst Achille's occupation was a Fruit Salesman. All three had by now married and had started families.

King Street (though later in 1935). No.19 is the white house in the far distance. Courtesy of Local Studies, Southampton Central Library.

In 1985, I recorded some memories of Achille's and Trofimena's second son, Carlo, who was then aged almost 77 years. He told me:

"King Street was in a poor locality. All the houses were small. There was a corn merchants in the street and a little jumble shop on the corner of Russell Street. At the top of East Street there was a grain store and we used to watch them pull the sacks up with a rope to the top floor in those days. In King Street we had four rooms, two up and two down. We had no garden in those days - there was a passageway at the side of the house leading to a yard which was Dad's store and where he kept his pony overnight. He used to go around here, and Totton and Lyndhurst, with a pony and cart, selling vegetables."

"A funny thing which my father did after he had sold the vegetables on the trap was to lie down on the tray underneath the trap and have a sleep. When he woke up he would find that he was back in King Street because the pony knew the way home. We had no shop when we lived in King Street - just living quarters and a pony and trap. Later we moved to Canal Walk, and that was a shop. Dad's older brother, Uncle Carlo was here too. (Born 1878). He had a fruit shop in East Street. When bananas came in they were green and he used to ripen them by heating his cellar. In those days he was called the 'Banana King'. My father had another brother in London". (Nicolo, born 1877).

East Street looking west 1909. Courtesy Local Studies, Southampton Central Library.

Canal Walk was also known as 'the Ditches'. In medieval times it was a defensive trench outside the fortifications of the town. In the late 18th century the building of a canal was initiated to establish a waterway link from Southampton to Winchester. This was a commercial venture that was never completed and eventually failed. By the early 19th century it was filled in and became a 'pleasant walk' on the semi-rural outskirts of the Georgian Spa town that was Southampton. Neighbouring Orchard Lane was also a 'delight'.

By 1850 genteel 'businesses with dwellings above' had been built and it was named Canal Walk. However, towards the end of that century shops began to appear and Canal Walk's air of respectability declined. Eventually, several 'lock-up' shops developed. Many of these were essentially small stalls with fold-up counters. Consequently, the rateable value of Canal Walk became a fraction of its commercial near-neighbours, East Street, Below Bar and High Street.

Bustling Canal Walk, early 20th century. Courtesy Local Studies, Southampton Central Library.

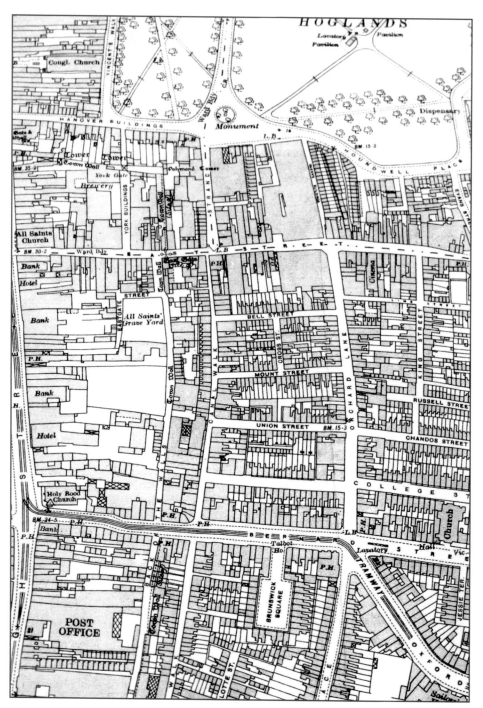

Section of street map of old Southampton from below Bargate in High Street to Oxford Street. Surveyed in 1865-67, revised in 1931-32. The Donnarumma Ice Cream Parlour was in the block of shops between Bell Street and Mount Street, along Canal Walk. Courtesy of City Archives, Southampton.

With its close proximity to the Docks, Canal Walk began to adopt a cosmopolitan, multi-cultural identity since it was an ideal place for immigrants arriving by sea to shop and eat. It was also a practical, affordable place for immigrants to set up shop. Thousands of immigrants from Italy, Russia, Poland, Germany and Eastern Europe lived temporarily at the Emigrants' Home Lodging House in nearby Albert Road whilst they were awaiting their allocation to sail on to America or other countries. The Jewish Rothschild family, with John Doling and his wife as Managers, founded this establishment which in 1908 was re-named the Atlantic Hotel.

Rumours of theft and vice in the area gave residents of Southampton a poor impression of the immigrant community though to the local British these appeared unfounded. Comedian, Tommy Cooper, born in 1921, started his career entertaining in Chiari's Ice Cream Parlour in Canal Walk. In 1924 Benny Hill was born nearby at what is now 111 Bernard Street. His parents' home at that time was above a lamp shop at this address. His father, Alfred, was the manager of the notorious surgical appliance shop called Stanley and Company which sold the contraceptives of the day, many by mail order. It was on the corner of Canal Walk and Mount Street, in close proximity to the Donnarumma Ice Cream Parlour. Film producer, Ken Russell was born in Southampton in 1927. His parents ran a shoe shop in a road off St Mary's Street which was also close to Canal Walk.

The Kelly's Directory of Southampton records number 14 Canal Walk as being in use as a shop of varying trades or for commercial use as far back as 1834 and possibly before. In 1911/12 it was run for a short time as a greengrocers by an Italian called Somona Gastano. However, by 1913/14 Achille Donnarumma was the proprietor and he too was a greengrocer though he later made ice cream at the back of the shop and in the back yard.

Canal Walk in rain at dusk. 1909. Courtesy City Archives Southampton Civic Centre.

Carlo described the area -

"Canal Walk was a street filled with shops - Jews, Italians, butchers, grocery shops, clothes shops, cat-meat shops, newsagents, shops selling cockles and whelks and ice cream. Our living quarters were at the back and above the shop. We had a kitchen-diner and a little scullery where we could wash up. We had a big store, upstairs and downstairs. On the walls we had pictures of family and friends of my parents in Italy. There was a big picture of my father with his pony and trap as well. That got lost during the Blitz. We had two front bedrooms and two at the back. We had a toilet but no bathroom. We used to bath in front of the fire in a tin bath. There was lino on the floor and no heating. Lighting was by a gas mantle on the wall. We got into bed with cold sheets although we had stone hot-water bottles - no rubber ones in those days!"

"When my mother had done the washing she used to dry it upstairs on long, inside washing lines. We had a little outside yard but nowhere to hang any clothes to dry. Every Monday morning we used to light the copper in the outside yard for Mother and she would wash by hand, boil and then hang up the clothes. Hard work in those days. The metal copper had a brick surround and we would light the fire underneath it to keep the water boiling. The washing came out beautiful - lovely and white. All done by hand."

"The cooking was done in the scullery. Before we had a gas cooker Mother used to cook on the top of an old range using iron saucepans. The old-fashioned iron kettle boiled away all day, mostly to make coffee. Real good coffee, not the powdered stuff you get today. We could tell the difference, even in those days. Most Italian families drank coffee although they were also fond of tea. We mostly ate macaroni, spaghetti or pasta, all bought in from Italy. My mother cooked a special meal with macaroni and beans which we called 'pasta vasoo'. It was really beautiful and filling. We sometimes had roast beef on a Sunday. Mother prepared it in a big oval dish by laying the potatoes on the bottom, then onion and tomato, with the beef on top. We children were then told to take it to Raynor's Bakery on the corner of Union Street and they would charge sixpence (6d) to cook it in their big ovens along with all the neighbours' dishes, all labelled with a number. That's the only time we had roast beef - on a Sunday. Every other day it was pasta, pasta."

Children in Bell Street 1930's. Courtesy Local Studies, Southampton Central Library.

"When we lived in Canal Walk we used to play in Bell Street, Mount Street and Union Street or visit different streets to play with other children who went to our school. The streets were very poorly surfaced but hard although East Street had 'tarmac'. Sometimes we'd go paddling along the shore, or at Town Quay or at Central Station because the water in those days came right up to the station. There was a wall to sit on. It wasn't a proper beach, it was stony but you could paddle. There was a boat-yard under the archway at the bottom of Westgate where we would go and sit to watch the boats. There was a jetty next to the Royal Pier where we would go fishing or crabbing. We used to catch the crabs from under the rocks and cook them in a tin on the quay."

"We sometimes went to the park opposite Edwin Jones' shop (now Debenham's department store) to play cricket, football or fly our kites. In those days you couldn't get into the cricket park for kites – everybody flew kites. You would have a job to get a space. It's a funny way we used to make them. We had some old-fashioned chest of drawers upstairs built into the wall. We used to pull the drawers out and cut the wood from the back. We could split the wood and make a lovely kite; or we could go and buy one for a penny (1d) or tuppence (2d) in South Front where a man used to make them and sell them. We preferred to make our own. A man called Gussie Shute from South Front made beautiful toy steam engines run by methylated spirits, though I didn't have one. Another man, a friend, Archie Reid, who had one leg and made good models also ran an amateur cinematogram in his back copper-house (wash house) where we would go to watch films. The cinema at the bottom of East Street was fun. We would go to watch cowboys, Tom Mix, and Rudy Valentino. There were no 'talkies', just a lady playing the piano and a man playing a violin as the film was shown. We used to have great fun in those days."

Children playing at Platform Quay 1922. Courtesy of City Archives, Southampton.

"I went to St. Joseph's School in Bugle Street. The Girls' section was in St. Michael's Square. Before we went to school Mother used to give us a ha'penny (half 1d) and we used to buy a 'happeth' of stale cake on the way. There was a baker's shop next door to the Holyrood Church where all the children bought stale cake on the way to school. We'd come home for lunch and then back to school. After school we used to go to play football in Westgate Street by the Old Walls to a place we called Mother Maisey's. (the site of West Gate House, Madame Maes' once beautiful Georgian home and gardens). We used to climb the steps and look out over the Docks and the nice sights. I stayed at St. Joseph's School until I left school at fourteen."

West Quay from the water looking back at West Gate, the town walls and Pickett's Boatyard. C.1910. Courtesy of Local Studies, Southampton Central Library.

CHAPTER 4
The 1st World War

It was not until April 1915 that Italy entered the 1st World War on the side of the Triple Entente - Britain, France and Russia. Achille Donnarumma was then 35 years of age and an Italian national. In mid 1915 Achille went off to War in Italy and by 1918 at the end of the War, 600,000 Italians had lost their lives, 950,000 were wounded and 250,000 were disabled for life, so it was with some luck that Achille returned safely.

During the 1st World War the Dolomites and Julian Alps were the areas of intense fighting between Italian and Austro-Hungarian troops. Many more succumbed to frostbite and avalanches than to bullets. In this 'Alpine Campaign' against the Austro-Hungarian Empire the Italians were initially defeated at the Battle of Caporetto in 1917. However, in 1918 the British, French and Italians were the victors at Vittorio Veneto. Carlo, Achille's second son remembered:

"I was only about eight years old when my father went away to the 1st World War. All I remember is him being dressed up in the green Italian Army uniform, with his putties. He wasn't actually a serviceman, he was a cook. My father was away until 1918. He used to tell us the stories of when he went up into the Alps to fight. Different fighting in those days. His older brother didn't go, I don't know why."

Achille Donnarumma in Italian Army uniform for 1st World War. Mid 1915.
Taken in Express Studies, Canal Walk. Courtesy of Brian Donnarumma.

Achille's older brother Carlo was not fit enough to join the Italian Army since he was suffering from a disease of the kidneys possibly contracted from a virus as a child in Italy, resulting in his death at the young age of 45 years in 1923, leaving a young wife, Norah Amelia (nee Ryan) and six children. Young widowed Norah later married Achille's eldest son, Nicolo and they had a further five children who survived. In 2010 I recorded the life of one of these children, Stella Wilde (nee Donnarumma) who was born in 1930. Stella told me:

> "My mother's first husband died at a young age. Mother had a picture of the funeral going up The Avenue. There were big black horses with plumes on their heads pulling the coffin carriage. It was a very big funeral because he was quite a prominent person with a shop in East Street. I think my mother ran the shop for a couple of years after his death in 1923."

For the time that Achille was away in the 1st World War serving in the Italian Army, Trofimena Donnarumma ran the vegetable and fruit shop at 14 Canal Walk, possibly with help from young Italian lodgers. She gave birth to their seventh child, Francesco, after Achille had left for Italy. She registered his birth signing with an 'x'. Their second child Carlo related:

> "My mother carried on the business. She worked very, very hard. Competition was fierce. I remember Mother visiting Uncle Carlo's shop in East Street and other shops. When she returned she would reduce the price of her produce so as to undercut him. (Author's note - other members of the family believe it was Carlo who reduced his prices after advising Trofimena to put hers higher). We all worked in the shop when we got home from school. My sisters too. We all worked very hard."

Domenic, Clotilda (Goodie), Amalia (Emily) and Eleanora (Yana).
Express Studio Canal Walk. Mid 1915. Courtesy of John Richardson

Trofimena standing, with her sister sitting (details unknown) and Emily and Clotilda. Express
Studio Canal Walk Mid 1915. Courtesy of Oral History Collection, City Archives, Southampton.

CHAPTER 5

Ice Cream Parlour and Refreshment Rooms, 13 and 14 Canal Walk, Southampton.

Although Achille Donnarumma was the proprietor of the fruit and greengrocer's shop at 14 Canal Walk from 1913 or 1914, he also sold Italian produce and made ice cream on these premises, where the whole family lived. Carlo told me:-

"We sold macaroni, spaghetti, pasta - all bought in from Italy. In those days the macaroni and spaghetti came in long boxes and we used to weigh it out for the customers - not pre-packed like today. My father also sold bottles of wine - Chianti. We sold a lot of brown kidney beans. We never sold coffee in our shop but we used to go to Ridgeway's in the High Street where they would grind the beans. It was lovely coffee. We also sold other continental goods such as olives, olive oil, garlic and everything you could think of for our continental Italian customers."

"We started making ice cream in the fruit and vegetable shop and sold it from there. Ha'penny (half 1d) for a cornet or a penny (1d) for a wafer, or people would come with their mugs to be filled with a penneth (ld or a penny) of ice cream to have with their dinner. In those days you got a lot of ice cream for a penny (1d)."

"We made the ice cream in a store at the back of the fruit shop. It was all made by hand in those days. We used ice and freezing salt. We had a wooden tub with a zinc container in which we put the ice cream mixture. We turned it by hand until it became hard. We had a long paddle with a zinc scraper and we used to scrape the ice cream off the sides of the zinc container. When it became hard we then packed it and it was ready for use."

"My brothers, Nicolo and Domenic and I used to go to Gough's Ice Store in Canute Road and pick up one hundred-weight blocks of ice on a specially made cart which could carry nearly half a ton. I remember once when Nicolo and I went to Gough's and we picked up eight hundred-weight of ice on this truck and pushed it all the way home. Almost half a ton of ice - that's hardly believable today but the ice block sat there and never moved and we could push it quite easily. For unloading we just slid it out. The platform was about a foot off the ground and we'd place a piece of wood to act as a slide. We'd then tip the cart and the block of ice would slide right out onto the pavement. Quite simple. We had big ice clippers and we'd drag the blocks right through the shop. Later we had a mosaic and marble floor, so the floor didn't become damaged. We'd take it out to the store where father had dug a big trench and we'd tip the ice block into it to stop it from melting. When any ice was required we just used the clippers and pulled some out."

Trofimena with Eleanora, Clotilda and Amalia. Ice Cream Parlour, Canal Walk mid 1920's.
Courtesy of Oral History Collection, City Archives, Southampton.

"We also used to sell ice cream in those days at 'The Fairs' on Southampton Common and we'd work all night long preparing it. We worked hard. They don't know what hard work is today."

Carlo standing, with Clotilda and friend outside Ice Cream Parlour, Canal Walk. Mid 1920's.
Courtesy of Oral History Collection, City Archives, Southampton.

Next door to 14 Canal Walk was a public house called the Horse Shoe Tavern which dated back to the 1850s and was on the corner of Brick Court and Canal Walk. The pub was refused a licence in 1920 because the Authorities felt there were too many pubs in close proximity. Marston's Brewery received £1,604 in compensation. Mrs Sarah Moody who had been the tenant for twelve years received £166 and 5 shillings. According to Kelly's Directory of Southampton this was number 13 Canal Walk and around 1923 Achille acquired this.

Canal Walk, Angel Corner Surplus Stores, 1920's. Courtesy of City Archives, Southampton.

Carlo continued:

"After ten years running the shop, Mum and Dad decided to develop an ice cream parlour and refreshment rooms. When the Horse Shoe Inn next door became vacant they acquired it. Dad did a lot of work on it and by about 1925 he had altered the front by putting in big folding doors making numbers 13 and 14 Canal Walk into one property. I remember we had a mosaic floor of marble and cement and it was really a lovely place. We had big long mirrors in the shop, marble-topped tables and a long counter with a big boiler for making teas, coffees and Oxo's."

Trofimena with her seven children, left to right, Nicolo, Carlo, Domenic, Eleanora (Yana), Clotilda (Goodie), Amalia (Emily) and Francesco (Babe or Francis) C1926. Courtesy of Stella Wilde (nee Donnarumma).

"Later Dad bought a mechanical ice cream maker run by electricity. It was much easier to make the ice cream using the same method but not having to turn by hand. The milk was delivered in churns by Southern County Dairies from their dairy at the bottom of the High Street. Father used to boil this milk over a gas stove to kill any bacteria. He boiled it all day long in four-gallon containers. After boiling the milk we then coloured it to make it look creamy like Cornish ice cream. We then flavoured it with vanilla, raspberry, chocolate or strawberry. We also used red cochineal to colour it. We never made coffee ice cream in those days. We worked very hard and we sold and sold and sold."

"Ice cream makers were very popular in those days. Chiari's and Pagliari's ice cream shops were further along Canal Walk. We all did good business because it was cheap. Our parlour opened at nine o'clock in the morning and closed at eight o'clock at night, selling all the time. We were even open on Sundays. No days off in those days. The only time my mother and father had off was when they went to Italy on holiday in the winter."

Trofimena Donnarumma with unidentified friend or relative,
interior of ice cream parlour. Late 1920's. Courtesy of Elise
Edwards (nee Donnarumma).

After combining 13 and 14 Canal Walk, Achille and Trofimena
originally named their shop 'Canal Walk Ice Cream Stores'.

Emily with two customers leaning on Ice Cream Parlour window, mid 1920's. Courtesy of Oral History Collection, City Archives, Southampton.

The period from 1920-1939 can be described as the 'Golden Era' for many Italians in Britain, especially for the 'old' immigrants – 'la vecchia emigrazione'. They had arrived before or just after the turn of the century, had worked hard and prospered. This was due to family cohesion and the fact that they were unaffected by the Depression because they were self-employed, owning service businesses. Some could now afford more frequent visits to the 'old country' and they built lavish villas in their villages or towns with the nostalgic intention of returning after retirement. Indeed, Achille and Trofimena bought a many-roomed villa near Sorrento in the San Michaela district, it is believed. It was let as seven separate apartments though Trofimena did not live there on her permanent return to Minori in 1939. The villa was not sold until after the death of Trofimena in Minori on 10th January 1963.

It was during this 'Golden Era' in Britain that Italian businesses called 'ice cream parlours' and 'refreshment rooms' developed in cities, towns and in coastal locations where holiday-makers or day trippers became their clientele. They varied in size and elegance and not only served ice cream but light foods and confectionery. They served cups of Bovril, Oxo, Tea and sold cigarettes. The ice cream parlours became social meeting points for friends, family and single young people. They were able to attract women and children, unlike the bars of the public houses. With long opening hours and some with the provision of music, they became popular with a wide range of the population, not only the Italians themselves. As Carlo told me:

"People used to come from miles away in those days. It was very good business. East Street, Canal Walk and the other streets with shops used to get packed with people. Everybody came there to walk up and down, up and down. On Sunday afternoons the younger generation used to come to our shop. We had a piano in the back and a radiogram in the front. They all used to come for the ice cream, teas, lemonade and pastry, whatever they wanted. Ha'penny (half 1d) for an ice cream, penny (1d) for a cup of tea or coffee and tuppence (2d - two pence) for a cake. The ice cream was very good."

Emily, Domenic and Clotilda. Ice Cream Parlour, Canal Walk. C.1926. Courtesy of Oral History Collection, City Archives, Southampton.

Eleanora and Clotilda by sign board at Ice Cream Parlour, Canal Walk. C.1926. Courtesy of Oral History Collection, City Archives, Southampton.

Canal Walk was also known as 'The Ditches'. Maie Hodgson in her book entitled 'Child of the Ditches' comments about the Donnarumma family thus:

"Next to the bakery in Canal Walk was Donnarumma's spacious spotlessly clean tea-room and ice-cream parlour. Aspidistras, lush and green on high pedestals were a permanent embellishment, and when it rained the matriarch of this lovable Italian family, would take the plants from their stands and place them in the little gully running through the centre of the Ditches till they'd had their fill. In the summer the large windows were folded back and the big churns of ice-cream were put outside. We kept a beady eye out for Goodie when we had a penny to spend because she would always make us a tu'penny wafer and similarly a penny cornet when all we had was a ha'penny (half-penny). Mrs Donnarumma was quite fond of my mother and although she spoke little English, they communicated easily by lots of hand movements and facial expressions. Many a time she would visit our shop with a little taster of one of their special batches of ice cream. These were usually made with real cream and sometimes contained fresh strawberries. Once she presented her with a glass jar of black cherries soaking in brandy."

'Child of the Ditches' by Maie Hodgson. Fleetwood Print, Southampton 1992.

Trofimena Donnarumma, Ice Cream Parlour, Canal Walk C.1925.
Courtesy of Oral History Collection, City Archives, Southampton.

Canal Walk approaching Bernard Street junction, looking south down Canal Walk. C.1920's.
Courtesy of City Archives, Southampton.

CHAPTER 6
The Donnarumma Music

Carlo was proud to tell me:

"My brothers Nicolo and Domenic played piano accordions and set up their own band, 'The Donnarumma Brothers' and then 'The Donnarumma Four'. Charlie Grover played the drums and Eileen Rhiordan was the vocalist. They were very popular and many people came to our Ice Cream Parlour to listen to them. I remember, every Saturday night we used to get packed out with people. They also played around the local pubs and even at the elegant Tivoli Hotel in the High Street. At times Billy Read's brother, John played the piano."

The Donnarumma Brothers Band and Artists appearing nightly at The Tivoli Hotel, Above Bar, Southampton. Courtesy of Brian Donnarumma

The Tivoli Restaurant first opened at 15 Above Bar (High Street) in 1898 by the Swiss-German Schumi family. During the 1920's the restaurant was converted to an hotel with a restaurant, bar, dance floor and entertainment. The Donnarumma Four became one of its resident dance bands. Sadly, it was destroyed in the German bombing of Southampton in the 2nd World War.

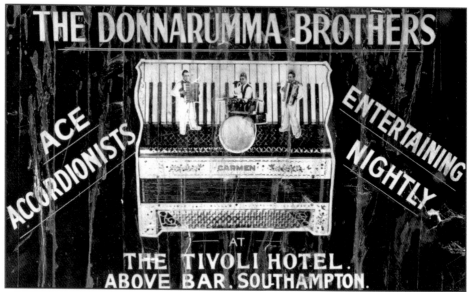

Poster advertising the Donnarumma Brothers. Courtesy of Elise Edwards (nee Donnarumma)

Stella, Nicolo's third child told me:

"My grandfather (Achille) we called 'Uncle Aggie' – I don't know why. Perhaps it was because he was actually an uncle to my older half brothers and sisters. We were all very close even though we had different fathers. We never alluded to 'half brother' or 'half sister'. It was always 'my brother' or 'my sister'. We called our grandmother (Trofimena) 'Mamai'. They spoke to one another in Italian but not to us grandchildren. He could speak more English than Mamai and I think they taught their children to speak Italian."

"Uncle Aggie and Mamai lived in Canal Walk. It was also called 'The Ditches'. They opened the first Ice Cream Parlour in Southampton. That's why he became very popular, well-known and memorable to this day. It seemed to me at my young age quite large, with a big glass frontage. It was very, very clean and a little bit austere. I remember the floor was beautiful. There were lovely tiles on the floor which were a mosaic pattern of blue and white. They stood out and were really lovely."

Buskers from London play with the Donnarumma Band, inside Ice Cream Parlour, Canal Walk, 1920s. Courtesy of Oral History Collection, City Archives, Southampton.

"I can remember Uncle Aggie making the ice cream at the back and bringing it through to be served, though I was never actually there when he made it. They served snacks, tea and fruit drinks too. We used to visit on a Sunday morning and have an ice cream. We'd catch the Woolston ferry to Southampton and walk up to Canal Walk."

Buskers from London play with the Donnarumma Band, inside Ice Cream Parlour, Canal Walk 1920s (Nicolo with piano accordion). Courtesy of Oral History Collection, City Archives, Southampton.

"I also used to sometimes watch my father, Nicolo, practising playing with the 'Donnarumma Four'. They rehearsed at the Tivoli Hotel in the High Street but sometimes in the Ice Cream Parlour. My father, Nicolo played accordion. His brother, Domenic also played accordion though he could play piano too. The drummer was Charlie Grover. He wasn't related but they were very close. Irene Rhiordan was the singer. She was beautiful and had a good voice. As far as I know, none of them read music. I can't ever remember any music in the house. If somebody hummed a song, they could play it. They played in clubs and pubs and at the Tivoli Hotel and became quite well-known. They dressed alike in costumes for their shows."

The Donnarumma Four on stage at The Tivoli Hotel, High Street, Southampton. 1939. Left to right: Mr Target (Manager of Tivoli), Domenic Donnarumma, Eileen Rhiordan, Charles Grover, Nicolo Donnarumma, Mrs Target. Courtesy of Oral History Collection, City Archives, Southampton.

"I can remember I went to see the Donnarumma Brothers take part in a talent show that was broadcast on the radio. It was called the Carroll Levis Musical Discoveries show. This episode took part on the Isle of Wight where there must have been a studio. We went on what seemed a huge ship though it was just a ferry, and I sat in the audience whilst they played. The rest of the family were at home listening to it on the radio".

"One tune they played was called 'Caravan' and I still love that tune to this day. They didn't win, they came second but it was really exciting to sit and watch them. They just knew each others' nods and movements and when to come in and what improvisations to make with their accordions. And they would always be laughing. They were always so happy. It really was a lovely time of my life. This was in 1937 or 1938 when I was only about seven or eight."

Domenic Donnarumma on right, with friend, playing accordions. 1930's.
Courtesy of John Richardson.

Talent scout and impresario, Carroll Levis (1910-1968) was a Canadian expatriate who came to Britain in 1935. He hosted amateur talent shows by first interviewing and auditioning. The shows were broadcast on BBC radio and at one time had a listening audience of over twenty million. Carroll Levis produced well-known phrases such as "The new and unknown artists of today are truly the stars of tomorrow". Countless contestants tried for stardom and big cash prizes when they played live on stage at various theatres and studios throughout the country. The shows were called "The Carroll Levis Musical Discoveries" and later "Reprise", then "Brass Monkey" and "Lucky Mascot". Carroll Levis entertained the troops in the second World War and continued his amateur talent programmes into the television era. It is reputed that John Lennon, Paul McCartney and George Harrison were to have been auditioned by Carroll Levis playing under the name of 'Johnny and the Moondogs' but they had to catch a last train home from the venue so never did get on the show.

Stella Donnarumma met her husband Victor Wilde when they were both working for Charles Forte at the 'Puritan Maid' in Piccadilly, London. Stella had worked there as a Waitress for some time before Victor arrived as a Manager. They married in Caxton Hall in July 1952 and held their reception at the Criterion Restaurant which was above the Puritan Maid. This was courtesy of the owner, Charles Forte, who also loaned the couple his chauffeur-driven car for the occasion. Stella and Victor were married for almost fifty years and they had one daughter, Linda (now Cadier) who is the Senior Advisor for LLAS-Centre for Languages, Linguistics and Area Studies at Southampton University. Victor died in 2001. Charles Forte was an Italian who created a worldwide empire of restaurants, hotels and other businesses from virtually nothing. Charles Forte died in 2007.

Stella Wilde (nee Donnarumma). 2010.

CHAPTER 7
Carlo Grows Up and Achille's Death in London

"I left school at fourteen in 1922 and worked in my parents shop but I decided it would be best for me to go out to work because there were so many of us at home. The first job I took was at Chattis Hill Racing Stables at Stockbridge. We knew the chef and his wife very well. He was a local man and his wife came from Brunswick Square in Southampton. There were young boy apprentice jockeys and horse trainers at Chattis Hill. My job was to look after the dormitory for about twenty boys as well as to help prepare the vegetables and other kitchen work. That's what I did, day in and day out, all day long, with probably an hour off in the afternoon. In the evenings I helped prepare the dinners and cleared the dishes. On my one day off a week I used to walk to the station and catch a train to Central Station, Southampton. I'd spend the day at home and then go back that night. Eventually, by 1927 I decided to leave this job and went home."

"My father said to me 'Carlo, the chef on the Berengaria has been here. He said, if you'd like to go down to the Docks and see him, he'll give you a job'. So I got a job on the Berengaria as Assistant Cook. Quite an easy job it was. As Assistant Cook I didn't do much cooking. I did that for a year and then got the job of Assistant Grill Cook. One of my jobs was to peel sides of bacon, bone them and cut them into rashers on a bacon machine. Everything was cut by hand in those days. There was never any pre-packed foods."

Carlo Donnarumma sitting in back yard of Ice Cream Parlour, Canal Walk 1920s.
Courtesy of Oral History Collection, City Archives, Southampton.

"After that I stayed at home at the Ice Cream Parlour and Refreshment Rooms but worked each day for the London and Southern Wholesale Company in West Quay Road opposite the Harbour Board offices. That's where their store was. I worked there for a number of years. I married Thora. We've now been married for fifty-four years. She's such a good woman. She would help anyone. We had three lovely children, Marie, Rita and Anthony who was born in 1938."

Berengaria cricket team 1929. Carlo Donnarumma third from left, middle row. Courtesy of Oral History Collection, City Archives, Southampton.

Thora Searles was an attractive local English girl who married Carlo in 1931. Stella told me:

"I can remember my mother was great friends with Carlo's wife, Auntie Thora. When she visited she often had on a spotted dress, little clutch bag and beret. She was always very fashionable. I used to look at her and think 'Oh, you're so beautiful'. Uncle Carlo must have thought so too because he married her. She was so lovely."

Carlo Donnarumma and Thora Searles in their courting days, late 1920's. Standing outside of shop front next door to Ice Cream Parlour, Canal Walk. Courtesy of Oral History Collection, City Archives, Southampton.

Carlo continued:

"After our marriage I went back to sea but on a smaller ship as Assistant Baker. We worked much of the night making the bread for the next day. On one trip our ship called in at Naples and I met my father who was there on holiday. True; I was asleep at the time and one of my friends came to my cabin and said 'Carlo, your dad's on deck'. I went up in my working clothes which he didn't like and told me to change. After I'd changed he took me out for the day. We went to a restaurant and had a beautiful meal. I remember that Mussolini was in power at the time and his photograph was on the wall of the restaurant. I said 'There's old Mussolini, Dad'. He said to me 'Shush, shush, be quiet, be quiet. You mustn't mention his name'. Yes, it's true. Anyway, Dad took me round the city of Naples all day and I sailed the next day and went to Palermo, Sicily. Dad said to me 'Would you like me to come to Palermo and I'll take you out again?' I told him 'No, don't bother Dad, we're only there for a day'. It seemed such a bother for him to have to catch a ferry there just for a day."

In the late 1920's Achille and Trofimena's marriage sadly came under strain. Trofimena therefore spent more time visiting and living in Minori. Since her arrival in England she had never really adapted to the inclement weather. Achille was mainly running the Ice Cream Parlour, which in around 1938 he re-named D'Orsay Refreshment Rooms. Their seven children had all grown up and the majority had married – all to English spouses, and there were some grandchildren.

Trofimena Donnarumma with grandson, John Richardson. Minori 1935 or 1936. Courtesy of John Richardson.

In May 1939 Achille died suddenly whilst staying at a hotel at 73 Oakley Square near Mornington Crescent, St Pancras in London. He might well have been a member of the Associazione Nazionale Combattenti, a club founded in 1919 for Italian veterans of the 1st World War. He might also have been a member of the Frattelanza Club or perhaps the Mazzini Garibaldi Club - both with branches in Clerkenwell. These clubs, and others, were social hubs for Italians. Some had plush environments and catered for an extensive cross-section of the Italian community. Sadly, most of these clubs eventually became affiliated to the Italian Fasci movement. Mussolini had been clever in his support of Italian expatriates in Britain and funded the Italian clubs to supply free Italian language evening schools, British seaside holidays for Italian immigrant children, a school for young musicians, a separate women's section, and many special events. It is therefore not difficult to imagine that many Italians living in Britain had little understanding of living under the rule of a dictator.

Achille Donnarumma was just 59 years old when he died in May 1939. It was the end of an era. Achille and Trofimena had progressed from very poor immigrants who had seven children to the owners of the successful Refreshment Rooms and Ice Cream Parlour, as well as owners of a large villa in Sorrento, Italy – their lives had seen vast changes – much of it built from their sheer hard work and that of their offspring.

Italian's Long Residence in Southampton

A well-known Southampton ice-cream manufacturer, Mr. Achelle Donnarumma, of Canal-walk, died in his sleep while in London. He was 59 years of age.

Mr. Donnarumma had been unwell for some time. He was a native of

MR. DONNARUMMA

Minori, in Salerno, Italy, and came to Southampton 42 years ago. He had not been in the town long before he had set up in business on his own, and it is claimed that he introduced the Italian method of making ice-cream into the town.

He had attended every fair on the Common for many years, as well as hundreds of fetes and garden parties.

He leaves seven grown-up children —four sons and three daughters—and 10 grandchildren.

Southampton newspaper Obituary article of Achille Donnarumma, May 1939. (In the last paragraph there is no mention of his wife). Southern Daily Echo, Southampton.

CHAPTER 8
The 2nd World War

The 2nd World War made a major impact on the life of Carlo's widowed mother, Trofimena Donnarumma. Benito Mussolini (1883-1945), who had come to power in 1922 had announced himself 'Il Duce', dictator of Italy by 1925. Mussolini had invaded Abyssinia (Ethiopia) in 1935 and declared an 'Italian Empire' by 1936. He provided military support, as did Hitler, to General Franco in the Spanish Civil War which had started in 1936 when he also signed an Agreement with Hitler. By 1939 Mussolini had also conquered Albania. In June 1940 Mussolini now declared war on Britain and France in the belief that the Fascists would soon be the victors and he would gain territories in the peace treaty that would follow, thus extending his 'Empire'.

From around 1936 hostility developed towards Italians living in Britain. By 1940 many Italians who had lived here for decades, though not taken British citizenship, became apprehensive for their safety and the continuation of their livelihoods. Some Italians Anglicized the names of their businesses and shops. Some even changed their surnames. For those who did not, or could not go back to Italy, the British government began a process of internment of Italian Fasci members followed by internment of selected Italian males between the ages of 17 and 60 who had been resident in Britain for less than 20 years. Internment then included some Italian females who lived close to British ports.

Trofimena Donnarumma hurriedly travelled to Southampton from Minori bringing her two grandsons, Tony Peden and John Richardson, British subjects who were staying with her. Trofimena, who had not taken British citizenship, did not stay long for fear of being interned.

Trofimena Donnarumma with her grandsons, John Richardson on left and Tony Peden on right. Italian passport document for returning grandsons to England dated 1938. Courtesy of John Richardson

Trofimena left behind all of her family. Three of her sons, Nicolo, Domenic, and Francesco, as British-born, were conscripted to the British Army. Her other son, Carlo, was serving in the Home Guard platoon and undertaking essential War work driving. Two of her daughters were conscripted to the ATS. (Auxiliary Territorial Service).

Clotilda (Goodie) Richardson (nee Donnarumma) in ATS uniform. Courtesy of John Richardson

Of Trofimena's nephews born in Southampton (sons of Carlo deceased 1923) Carline b.1912 was a ships' riveter doing essential War work; Geraldo b.1914 was serving on mine sweepers in the British Merchant Navy; Archie b.1915 was undertaking essential War work and Antonio b.1923 joined the Royal Navy. Her niece, Doris b.1916 was a nurse in the British Red Cross, and her other niece, Lucia b.1919 worked in the War Munitions factory (now Fords). Her grandson, Nicolo junior b.1926 (Brian Donnarumma's father) served in Burma and Singapore. Due to his young age this was towards the end of the War.

Carlo continued his story -

"After my time at sea the 2nd World War started in 1939. I was a lorry driver by then and I had a chance to get a job with the Hants and Dorset bus company as a driver. By that time we lived in a little temporary cottage on a farm at the bottom of Whinwhistle Road, West Wellow, near Romsey, Hampshire. During the War I collected workers in this area and took them mainly into Southampton Docks where they did essential War work. I brought them back on the bus to Wellow at night. I was also a member of the Wellow Home Guard platoon."

Trofimena's eldest son, Nicolo, served as a driver in the Royal Army Service Corp, first in North Africa and then in Italy where he arrived after the Battle of Salerno which had taken place in the Autumn of 1943. Carlo recalled:

"In 1959 when I went to Italy with my brother, Domenic, to see our mother she was telling us about the time when the Americans and British landed at Salerno during the War. She said from where she was she had a view right out over Salerno Bay and could see lots of tracer shells and bullets flying. She told us she was very hungry and had no food. All they ate were lemons, oranges, peaches, whatever was in season. It was a very hard time for them all. My brother, Nicolo, was a front-line petrol supply lorry driver for the British Army and he arrived after the Battle of Salerno. He knew our mother was nearby and he went to find her. He said she was in a bad way so he took her some Army food and spent seven days leave with her. It was even reported in the Southampton Echo here with a heading "In War brother meets brother but seldom a son meeting his mother.""

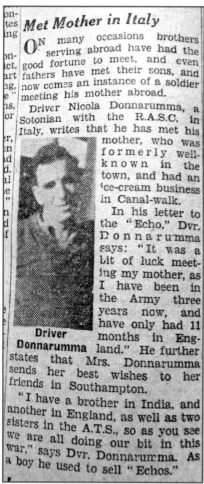

Met Mother in Italy

ON many occasions brothers serving abroad have had the good fortune to meet, and even fathers have met their sons, and now comes an instance of a soldier meeting his mother abroad.

Driver Nicola Donnarumma, a Sotonian with the R.A.S.C. in Italy, writes that he has met his mother, who was formerly well-known in the town, and had an ice-cream business in Canal-walk.

In his letter to the "Echo," Dvr. Donnarumma says: "It was a bit of luck meeting my mother, as I have been in the Army three years now, and have only had 11 months in England." He further states that Mrs. Donnarumma sends her best wishes to her friends in Southampton.

"I have a brother in India, and another in England, as well as two sisters in the A.T.S., so as you see we are all doing our bit in this war," says Dvr. Donnarumma. As a boy he used to sell "Echos."

Driver Donnarumma

Nicolo Donnarumma 'Met Mother in Italy' Southampton Newspaper Article dated 21st February 1945. Southern Daily Echo, Southampton.

Nicolo Donnarumma in British Army uniform back row with Italian relatives in Minori, 17th January 1945. Back row left to right: a friend, Francesca Esposito, Nicolo Donnarumma, Rosa Esposito. Front row left to right: Trofimena Esposito, child Andrea Lembo, Maria Esposito. The Espositos are sisters (Maria appears on page 110). Courtesy of John Richardson.

Trofimena's third son, Domenic served with the Royal Army Medical Corp in India. In his little spare time his music would have sustained him and helped him entertain the troops, as in the newspaper article opposite:

Domenic Donnarumma (seated with piano accordion) and Army friends. Newspaper article, 3rd August 1944. Southern Daily Echo, Southampton.

Three Sotonians Abroad

PRIVATE W. CROSS, R.A.M.C., and his two friends, Pte. Donnaruma and Pte. Ediss, serving in a British General Hospital in India, send an interesting letter and photograph of themselves. "It will be a big surprise to our wives and families," writes Pte. Cross. "We are three Sotonians who four years ago—October 1940—left the Central Station to join the Forces together."

Since then they have seen many lands and had many experiences. They left England in July 1941, with a R.A.M.C. canvas hospital, had a long sea voyage round the Cape, were attached to the Eighth Army in the desert—now they wear the African Star ribbon—

Pte. Cross and pals.

had another long sea voyage and are now attending wounded from the Burma front.

"At periods when Monty and the Eighth Army boys were all out we worked day and night taking under our canvas hospital thousands of patients, British, Poles, Indians—and parties of German and Italian prisoners—who needed medical treatment."

Pte. Cross also recalls an incident in the desert when on a moonlight night he and his pals were walking across the desert he chanced to pick up an old newspaper almost buried in the sands. "To our surprise," he writes, "it was an old edition of the "Echo" almost unreadable, but we could just see the date, showing February 1941."

"Pte. Donnaruma—seated with the piano accordion— was well-known with his accordion band in pre-war days at the Tivoli in Above Bar, and in many dance halls in Southampton" writes Pte. Cross. "He still makes time to keep in trim on the keys and entertain the boys and the patients at our hospital. In the centre of the group is "Sembo, our crooner from West Africa." Pte. Cross—in shorts—was a mem-

Advertising poster, Grand Dance at Coimbatore, Madras, India. 17th March 1944. Courtesy of Brian Donnarumma.

Stella Wilde (nee Donnarumma) the third child of Nicolo, was evacuated from Southampton and recalls:

> "We children were all enrolled to go to an evening school to learn to speak Italian. We were so excited because we were going to have a uniform for these lessons but war broke out and we never did get there. Instead, my brothers Nick, Ray, Mario and I were evacuated to Old Basing near Basingstoke. I think it was the 1st September 1939 when the coaches drew up outside St Patrick's Roman Catholic school in Woolston and took us to the Central railway station. Although I was nine I almost broke my heart on leaving my Dad at the station. However, I was billeted with a Mrs Brown and her daughters, Mary and Sylvia. My brothers were with other families. I was with my class-mate, Mary Foley. I was treated exactly like one of the family and they were amazing to me".

> "Our class teachers came too and taught us at General Maddox's country house which he had given up for that purpose. It was a lovely house with beautiful gardens. I was with the Brown family for almost five years, though I did spend the odd weekend back at home in Southampton and my mother came to visit me. I think I learnt a lot more at Old Basing and I was certainly cared for very well."

After the death of Achille Donnarumma in 1939 the Ice Cream Parlour, now known as "D'Orsay Refreshment Rooms" was run by one of his daughter's Amalia (Emily) together with her friend, Lois Violet D'Orsay (aka Dyer). The building was damaged during the Blitz of Southampton in November and December of 1940 along with many surrounding residential streets in this centre of old Southampton. After the War the building was acquired under a Compulsory Purchase Order and demolished together with all other war-torn buildings in the community. As many have said: 'What the slum clearance of 1935 had not finished, the Blitz completed in 1940'. New buildings were erected - the very end of an era.

There is a later Donnarumma Family Tree in Appendix II on page 120

11 Canal Walk after bomb damage. Courtesy City Archives, Southampton.

13 Canal Walk after bomb damage. Courtesy City Archives, Southampton.

CHAPTER 9

Carlo's Ice Cream at West Wellow and Trofimena's Death in Minori

Carlo's first ice cream van converted from an American Chrysler ambulance. Note on left the ex-Army radio communications trailer from 2nd WW which Carlo used for his stores. Left to right - Friend, Jackie Barter, Thora and Carlo Donnarumma, Stuart Pereira and Linda Pereira his mother. Dogs are Bruno (uncle's dog from London) and Rex. 1950.

In 1985 Carlo concluded by telling me:

"After the end of the War I decided I'd like to make ice cream again. It was difficult then to obtain sugar and enough milk and other ingredients for making the ice cream. We had to go to the Food Office and ask them if they would make us an allocation of sugar because we would like to start making ice cream. We were told 'no' they could not give us any sugar but if we could buy sweetened ice cream powder we could make it. We managed to get some and we started making ice cream here. At the time we had no electricity so we made it in a gallon tub but later we made it by machine and with the authentic ingredients from my family's recipe."

Carlo Donnarumma at his Ice Cream Stall, West Wellow, early 1980's. Peter G Murrell.

"We are still here today (1985) making the same ice cream as my father made in Canal Walk. We sell it from our bungalow every day in the summer but in winter just at weekends. Also, we have an ice cream van and my wife goes out on that around the Totton, Romsey and Calmore areas and around the villages. Mondays, Wednesdays and Fridays we go to a school playground in Romsey. My wife also goes to old-aged people's homes because they can't get out. She asks them what they would like and takes the ice cream inside to them. Our son, Tony works with us for three days a week in the summer. It's so good to know we are making the same ice cream as my father used to make."

ICE CREAM PRICES TO BE CONTROLLED

Food Front Gives "No Hopes" of Improvement

SIR BEN SMITH, new Minister of Food, to-day announced the immediate control of prices of ice cream.

Sold from barrows, over the counter, or in cafes, the price now charged must not exceed 50 per cent. more than was charged for similar portions of similar quality before the war. Control will apply to all classes of ice cream, including water ices, and to frozen substitutes for ice cream.

The order will not apply to ices included as part of an ordinary meal.

Asked whether he would do anything to improve the quality of ices, Sir Ben said: "I am not going to do anything to deflect either sugar or fat from the domestic table."

NO EXTRA RATIONS

Sir Ben, who was holding his first Press conference as Food Minister, declared: "There is no prospect of any improvement in the rations. The restoration of recent cuts is at the moment something for the future. It is too early to say what benefits we shall derive from the end of the Pacific War. Ultimately, if the shipping is available, the position should improve.

"First claims on rice will have to be for the rice-consuming peoples.

"There is little likelihood of substituting corned beef by carcass meat in the meat ration before the end of the year. The amount of canned meat available on points cannot be increased.

SUGAR ECONOMIES

"There is no hope at the moment of restoring the cuts in fats and bacon either to the domestic consumer or the manufacturer.

"We shall have to make further economies in the use of sugar, but I shall not reduce the domestic sugar ration below half a pound a week.

"Dried eggs will be issued on a lower scale, but more shell eggs should be available."

Sir Ben indicated that he could say nothing definite yet about an increase in the cheese ration.

NEW FISH PLAN

"This is not a cheerful picture, but I think it is right that the country should know the worst side of things," he said. "There is some slight relief in the increasing supplies of fish. From September 15 a new scheme of fish distribution to secure a fair share for all shops, but allowing the maximum flexibility in distribution from the ports is to be introduced.

TOMATOES—AND ORANGES

"There will be more tomatoes available soon.

"We shall have more oranges—and soon."

The Minister announced that, commencing from October 14, and continuing until March 30, there will be issues of household milk available throughout the winter at the rate of sufficient to make four pints of liquid milk per consumer in each eight week period. Although he could not give any definite assurance yet, he hoped that there would be more liquid milk available this winter.

"There is no real solution of the queue problem other than plentiful supplies and plentiful labour," he said.

Southern Daily Echo 14th August 1945.

Carlo Donnarumma with customers outside ice cream stall, West Wellow, Hampshire.

Carlo Donnarumma - out in all weathers, even the snow. January 1982. Courtesy of Southern Daily Echo.

Carlo's mother, Trofimena, continued to live in Minori after the War and as far as in known never returned to England. Before the War her youngest son, Francesco (Babe) had lived with her briefly and attended the last year of his schooling in Minori. Trofimena went back with him to England for his first job as a Bell Boy at the Crown Hotel, Southampton though they returned to Minori when Babe was 17 years, to enable him to take up a job at the Hotel Palumbo in Ravello in 1932. Trofimena's daughters visited periodically and her sons less frequently. They were busily involved with bringing up their own children and continental travel was not cheap. Her third son, Domenic, who had no children stayed with her most frequently. Trofimena eventually had fifteen grandchildren and one adopted grandson.

Trofimena Donnarumma with person possibly called Diana (details unknown) and kittens. Grandson, John, named the cat Belvedere. Minori 1950's. Courtesy of John Richardson. John stayed with his grandmother in Minori for his leave periods during the time he spent undertaking his National Service in Germany.

In January 1963, at the age of almost 83 years Trofimena died in Minori. Initially, as is the tradition, she had a grave with a marble cross engraved with her name. After a set period of years the remains are placed into a family wall vault. Trofimena's remains are probably buried in the Proto family vault, although some family members believe they are in the vault of Gennaro Lamberti and Castellano family. Trofimena's mother, Maria Proto, had the maiden surname of Lamberti.

Her family brought ice cream to Soton

THE death of an old Italian woman not far from Naples . . . and the end of a link in a family which brought ice cream to old Southampton.

Many Sotonians will remember the familiar ice cream tricycles which patrolled parts of pre-war Southampton.

A well-known business was that of the Donnarumma family — believed to be the first to sell Italian ice cream in Southampton.

They established a shop in the then familiar Canal Walk.

Eighty-three-year-old Mrs. Trefomena Donnarumma, who came to Southampton with her husband before the First World War, died where she was born—Minori, near Naples.

The "Echo" has been informed of her death by her grandson, Mr. Colin Donnarumma, who is with the Pendennis Castle.

FOUR-DAY JOURNEY

In October, 1959, Domenic and Carlo Donnarumma left Southampton to start a four-day car journey to Italy.

They went to visit their mother. Domenic (a blind pianist known in Southampton) and Carlo were two of the seven children born to Mr. and Mrs. Donnarumma after they had settled in Southampton.

'Misadventure' verdict on licensee

SOUTHAMPTON Borough Coroner Mr. D. H. B. Harfield recorded a verdict of "Death by misadventure" on Henry Charles Welstead (53), landlord of Ye Olde Trusty Servante, Minstead, New Forest, who died on his way to hospital at Southampton last Wednesday after falling down his cellar steps.

The Coroner said a pathologist's report had revealed that Mr Welstead had suffered from a heart complaint of which even he himself probably was unaware It could have produced a black-out leading to his fall down 11 brick steps, below which was a concrete cellar floor

His death was due to head injuries

SCRAP NOW

Metal Industries' two shipbreaking companies broke up eight tankers in 1962, totalling nearly 75.000 tons.

Newspaper Obituary article of Trofimena Donnarumma. January 1963.
Southern Daily Echo, Southampton.

The cemetery in Minori 2011.

Funeral procession of Trofimena Proto Donnarumma. Minori January 1963.
Courtesy of Elise Edwards (nee Donnarumma).

CHAPTER 10

Anthony Carlo Donnarumma's Era - Carlo's Ice Cream Parlour and the Death of Carlo and Thora

In 2008 I recorded the memories of Carlo and Thora's son, Anthony Carlo (Tony). His first memories were:

"My first memory of Wellow was of Canada Road. We moved out here from Totton where I was born. I was only about six months old when my Mum and Dad worked for the Hants and Dorset bus company. My Mum was the conductress and my Dad was the driver. They had to bring the bus out to West Wellow every night once we had moved here as they couldn't take it back to the station because of the bombing of Southampton. My Dad didn't go into the Army because he was a bus driver and that was an essential War work job taking the workers into the Docks each day."

"I've got one sister who is three years older than me, Rita, and I have another sister six years older than me, Marie. I was the baby of the family - the spoilt one! (born 1938). We lived in temporary accommodation in Canada Road but by the time I was five my parents were renting a new bungalow in Romsey Road for ten shillings a week. That was the bungalow here in West Wellow where you interviewed my father in 1985, where he made and sold ice cream. That's where I was brought up."

Bungalow, Ice Cream Stall and Ice Cream Van, West Wellow,
late 1970's. Courtesy of Wellow History Society.

"My parents were still working on the buses when, at weekends Dad used to make a little container of ice-cream. He hired a pony and trap from a man in the village called Mr Judd - he was a big, fat man. Dad would put this container on the pony and trap and Mum would go all around the village with a little bell and sign stating 'Stop me and buy one'."

"It started to get busier and busier so Dad bought an old American Chrysler ambulance. I think he paid about £50 for it. Two brothers, friends of Dad's who worked as coach builders at the Hants and Dorset Bus Company converted it into an ice-cream van and then Dad started to venture out into Totton, Nomansland, and places like that. So, weekends Mum and Dad used to go out on the van selling ice-cream and during the week they worked for Hants and Dorset Bus Company."

Ice cream van adapted from vehicle. 1939 Chrysler converted ambulance. Thora Donnarumma at rear, attending horse gymkhana at Paulett's Lane, Calmore, early 1950's.

Ice cream van adapted from vehicle. 1936 Ford Bedford, Carlo Donnarumma serving ice cream in Cheam Way, Testwood, 1952.

"My first memory I have of going out on the van was when Mum and Dad went to a Fete or Carnival and I'd go with them for a ride. It wasn't until later years that I used to help Mum serving on the van. By the time I was driving Mum around I would have been seventeen or eighteen. Also, later than that when I had left the sea, so I would probably have been about twenty-one then."

"When they stopped working on the buses Dad had a job in the Docks as an electrician's mate where he used to work nights. They then used to make ice cream and go out and sell it all day. So Dad would be working nights in the Docks and working day-times on the van selling ice-cream."

"My role in the making of the ice cream when I was a lad was to turn the gallon freezer. After Dad got the Chrysler van we used to go into Millbrook Rail Station near the Docks and pick up a hundred-weight slab of ice and bring it home. We used to chop it up into little bits and pack it round the freezer, plus put some salt around to make it freeze harder. I used to just turn and turn. It would take about twenty minutes to turn a gallon out. All by hand. We used to take it out and put it into a tub and then do another gallon. As long as the ice was wrapped up with sacks it used to last over a weekend. A hundred-weight block would last two or three days really."

Donnarumma brothers - left to right - Domenic, Carlo and Nicolo reminisce about pushing the hundred-weight ice blocks in the 1920's. Taken at Carlo's Ice Cream Stall, Romsey Road, West Wellow. 1970's. Courtesy of Stella Wilde (née Donnarumma).

"There was no electricity in the village at one time and my Dad had three poles put up at £60 each. After that my Dad got a proper shed and an electric machine but before that we also had a Lister engine, a water-run petrol engine, which turned the freezer. It had a belt which we greased with black treacle to stop it from slipping. When the ice-cream started to get hard the belt used to slip. When it was finished we'd go outside and turn the Lister engine off. We'd load up the big freezer and put it on the back of the van, push it up on a plank and pad it with ice and paper and salt. Then Mum and Dad used to go around the villages selling this ice-cream. We used to do chocolate, coffee, strawberry, cherry, raspberry, pineapple and vanilla. Not so many as I have now but that was about the range with Dad."

Carlo and Thora Donnarumma making ice cream, West Wellow, May 1976. Courtesy of Southern Daily Echo.

"Nothing ever worried my Dad. He worked very, very hard but he loved doing what he was doing. He was full of fun really. He was a great community man. Everybody loved Dad. Nobody ever had a bad word against him. Over the years Dad and Mum supplied gallons of ice cream for sale by charities and churches and have given unsold stock to orphanages and homes for handicapped children. Dad loved his Mercedes car and even chauffeured it for local weddings, providing the service for free."

Carlo Donnarumma acts as chauffeur with his much-loved Mercedes. Local wedding at St Margaret's Church, East Wellow.

"In 1985 my Dad and Mum received an invitation from the Lord Chamberlain to attend a Queen's garden party at Buckingham Palace. At first my Dad said he didn't want to go but I told him "Of course you have to go".

Carlo and Thora receive an invitation to Buckingham Palace, July 1985. Courtesy of Southern Daily Echo.

"So off they went to Buckingham Palace. They both had new teeth and new outfits. They were very eccentric people; they never used to dress up at all - but they did for the Queen. Even the local school closed down for the day and all the children came to wave good-bye to Carlo and Thora. We put up a sign 'Closed today because Carlo's gone to tea with the Queen'. Southern Television followed their car to London and, although rarely allowed, they were able to film my parents walking around the Buckingham Palace garden party."

Local children send off Carlo and Thora Donnarumma to Buckingham Palace - July 1985. Courtesy of Pat Sillence Archive, Lower Test Valley Archaeological Study Group (LTVAS), Romsey Town Hall.

Opening of Chapel and Northam Exhibition, July 1985. Tudor House Museum garden, Southampton. L to R: Barbara Donnarumma, Bill Smith, Eleanora Peden (Yana, nee Donnarumma), Eddie Peden, Carlo Donnarumma, Clotilda Smith (Goodie, nee Donnarumma), Rita Rogers (nee Donnarumma), Marie Martin (nee Donnarumma). Marie and Rita are Carlo's daughters.

Tony Donnarumma continued his story -

"I never saw one of my grandparents. Grandfather died in 1939 when I was one year old, so obviously I wouldn't remember him. My grandmother went back to Italy just before the 2nd World War, to Minori in southern Italy on the Amalfi Coast, between Salerno and Sorrento. My grandfather's name was Achille Donnarumma and he married a lady called Trofimena Proto in 1905. They had seven children, all born here. Nicolo was the eldest, then my Dad Carlo, then Domenic, then Eleanora, called Yana, Clotilda, called Goodie, Amalia, called Emily, and the youngest was a boy, Francesco, called Francis or 'Babe'. All seven children married English spouses."

"It seems strange to think that my grandmother lived in Southampton for thirty-four years but went back to her roots in Minori before the War and never returned to these shores again. Of course, she and my grandfather made regular visits to Minori over the years and had a large house near Sorrento I believe, though I never did see it, nor did most of the family. I think at the time of her death in 1963 she was living in a flat overlooking the bay of Minori. One of my cousins, Alfonse, still lives there (now deceased). He won some money on a Lottery and had a statue of St. Trofimena made in glass and had it placed on the Amalfi Drive highway in Minori."

Alfonse Esposito and Francesco (Babe) Donnarumma, Minori 1964 or 1965. Courtesy of Elise Edwards (nee Donnarumma).

"My first school was Wellow School. We had two class-rooms, a sandpit and that was it, apart from a little tarmac playground. I used to walk up the road to the school because there was no traffic in those days and we were safe. I stayed there until I was eleven and then I went to Bartley School at Cadnam. That was the senior school where I stayed until I was fifteen."

"When I left school I worked at the local farm for a month or so but I'd applied to Cunard for a job because I wanted to go away to sea. My Dad had been a sea-farer at one time in his life. Cunard sent me to Gloucestershire to a training ship called 'The Vindicatrix'. I joined the Catering Department but there were Seamanship courses held there too. We learnt the jobs of Ships Steward, Waiter, Silver Service, Kitchen Assistant and so on. The cost of the course was paid by Cunard and we wore a black uniform and cap. It was a really nice sea school."

"When I'd finished the course Cunard gave me a job as a Bellboy. I had a uniform of black trousers, red top, gloves and a pill-box hat. Cunard sent me to a ship called the 'Sythia' which was running to Quebec, Canada. I would say there were about 1,000 passengers. She wasn't a huge ship. That was my first trip as a Bellboy at sea but we hit a storm, a hurricane, and we were several days late arriving. I was so ill I said I would never go to sea again!"

"I left the 'Sythia' and said I wasn't going back to sea again but my Dad insisted and sent me to see a friend of his who worked for Cunard who said he had a nice little job for me. He used to call me 'Carlo's son'. The job was on the Queen Mary as a Bellboy. That was a different kettle of fish, a huge ship, 83,000 tons. That was the first Queen Mary. She is in Long Beach, California, now."

Anthony Donnarumma in his Bellboy uniform, with friend,
on railings of the liner Queen Mary. C.1955.

"I was paid two pounds and ten shillings a week with full board, plus tips. As a little English boy and very small, I got lots of tips. I used to open and shut the doors for passengers, rich film stars and so on and hand them boxes of matches and mints. I made a fortune in tips - but of course, young boys don't save! We were called 'Cunard Yanks'. We used to walk very proudly around Southampton with our Discharge Books in our top pockets to let the girls know that we were 'Cunard Yanks'! That was all the fun of growing up."

"When I was about eighteen there was an epidemic of what we called 'Asian flu' - that was about 1956. All the waiters were going down with it like flies and there was nobody to serve dinners so Cunard turned the Bellboys into Waiters. They took us off the doors and put us into the saloons. We had to put the food anywhere, so long as it went on the table! We weren't given more pay though."

Anthony Donnarumma serving passengers on board liner Queen Mary. 1956.

"I remember coming into New York at Pier 90. I thought it was wonderful. I still love it. I go back there now and take my wife, Barbara. Three or four days is enough for me because New York never sleeps. To see New York at Christmas-time or in the New Year, is beautiful. In the 1950's we were told not to use certain streets from 50th to 42nd to be safe. Above 50th you could be in trouble. It was in New York that I had my first real American burger and coconut milk shake. Of course, that's all gone now. We used to go to Broadway to listen to Louis Armstrong. We used to have lots of bands on board and they also played for the crew. We had Eric Delaney, Joe Loss, Ted Heath. They would come to the crew's Pig and Whistle and play for us. When Bill Hayley came on board he wouldn't play for the crew though."

"Later I was made a Commis-Waiter in First Class. I learnt the trade there. Every passenger wanted something different. Some of the people on board I remember were President Tito of Yugoslavia, the Queen Mother, Field Marshall Montgomery, Doris Day, Dick Powell, June Alyson. We took Don Cockle to New York to fight Rocky Marciano. When he came on board he was fit but coming back he was all bruised. I remember he brought a Cadillac car on board for his children. It was a model of a Cadillac and it was shipped on board in a big crate."

Anthony Donnarumma, Commis-Waiter, RMS Queen Mary. C.1956.

"After that I worked on the Queen Elizabeth. She was graceful, so graceful. In the First Class there were probably two waiters for two passengers. Passengers could have anything they wanted. That's why Cunard went bust because they gave the passengers too much. Caviar, or whatever, there was an abundance of food. The crew could have the same food. We used to pay a Chef who would cook for about five or six of us at the end of the evening. We would pay him about £20 a trip and he would provide anything we wanted."

"Working for the Union Castle Line on the Cape Town Castle was quite an eye-opener. Two weeks to Cape Town, Port Elizabeth, East London, Mussel Bay, Durban and back to pick up stores, and two weeks to get back. There were a lot of coloured men on board but they weren't allowed to sleep in our accommodation. They had to sleep on deck at night but they would load all the fruits, bananas or whatever."

Anthony Donnarumma on right, friend 'Blondie' on left. Table Mountain, Cape Town, 1957.

"I loved Durban. It was beautiful fifty years ago. Cape Town was also nice. We used to travel in rickshaws with coloured boys pulling us. They ran like horses. I didn't like the apartheid though. When we used to dock the black people would come down to the quay and rummage through the dustbins for bones and meat. I thought it wasn't right for people to have to live like that. However, when we went ashore we had to come back by taxi because the black people would be lying in wait and beat you up and strip you naked. They would steal anything but I could see their problem. They weren't allowed on buses or in cinemas. They had their own bars. It was a shame to treat people like that and I didn't believe in that."

"I met my wife, Barbara, in 1956 when she was quite young. Her father was a very good friend of my father. When Barbara knew I was home from sea she used to come to visit us with her Dad. It just lead from there really. I asked her to go out with me and we started courting. Her mother sometimes used to try to part us because she said she was too young. Everybody said 'It will never last'. We saved hard and Barbara was very good at 'bottom drawer' as well. We got married in 1959 so we will have been married for fifty years next year. We had a lovely wedding at Millbrook Church. By the end of 1959 I first left the sea. I did a couple of trips on the Cape boats and then I went onto the Queen Elizabeth as a Tourist Waiter but after that I packed up. When you get married you don't want to be away from your wife."

Anthony Donnarumma and Barbara Pound cutting their wedding cake.
Married at Millbrook Church, Southampton. July 1959.

"I got a job as a Thames trailer lorry driver but then went to work for the British Oxygen Company for about eleven years. I then worked for Westminster Dredging Company and travelled quite a bit here and around the world. Our daughter, Beverley was born in 1962 and our son, Anton (Anthony) in 1964 and we were buying our own house. By 1985 I was working for my Dad, making and selling ice cream, though only in the summer months. I was young and healthy and found it easy to get other winter work at that time."

Carlo (standing on box) and Anthony Donnarumma making ice cream
at West Wellow. 1970's. Courtesy of Wellow History Society.

"However, Dad started to get a bit old and asked me to help him full-time. I told him that he could not afford to pay me a proper wage, mostly because of the way in which he ran the business. For instance, he would often put up a sign 'Sorry sold out' at about three or four in the afternoon and he didn't keep bills or book-work in order. I told Dad that if he wanted me in, that Barbara, my wife, would do the book-work and we had to run the business properly; so he agreed."

Anthony Donnarumma with his father, Carlo, and mother, Thora
with ice cream van. West Wellow. Courtesy of Wellow History Society.

"When I was working for Dad, the traffic on this road here was getting so busy with people parking right down to the corner of Whinwhistle Road, so that they could come to buy our ice cream. The Police were starting to get annoyed. One Sunday they put up bollards to prevent any parking. I told them they couldn't stop a business from thriving and telephoned my MP who had the bollards removed straight away. We might have lost our business and Carlo's had been here all those years."

Carlo and Anthony Donnarumma pose for The Romsey Advertiser article on the need for off-road parking at Carlo's Ices, 1989. Courtesy of Pat Sillence Archive, Lower Test Valley Archaeological Study Group (LTVAS) Romsey Town Hall.

"This gave me the idea that if Barbara and I could buy the corner piece of land two doors down from where Mum and Dad lived, we could build a proper ice cream parlour, and with a lot of parking, which would be much better than what Dad had where there was no inside seating area. I approached the owners, who were farmers. I said to them 'If I can get building permission, can I buy this piece of ground from you?' They said 'Tony, you'll never get permission because this is a Green Belt area'. But I replied 'Give me a chance'. We made an agreement that if I got Planning Permission I would pay treble what it was worth as agricultural land."

Carlo Donnarumma. Carlo and Tony serving ice cream. Both photographs Courtesy of Wellow History Society.

"I submitted plans two or three times and they were turned down. At that time I noticed that our local MP had written in the local newspaper, the Echo, that he thought that one day someone was going to get killed outside of Carlo's because of the parking problem. I immediately telephoned the MP and told him of my plans and he advised me to re-submit them. In the end everybody was so happy to get the traffic off the road and my Planning Application was passed. This was in 1990 and the day the Planning Permission was passed, my Dad died, on the very day! He never knew but he had seen all the plans. Dad died in June 1990 aged 82 years."

The funeral of Carlo Donnarumma. St Margaret's Church, East Wellow, June 1990. Family members carry the coffin.

"We went to see our Bank Manager who wanted three years of trading figures, which of course, we didn't have because we hadn't yet built the business. Our children Beverley and Anton were married so we sold our house and moved a caravan with running water onto the site and from here Barbara organised everything. We were right next door to the building work. She phoned around for prices for bricks, cement and timber. She got the best prices. She was really switched on. Her estimate for the building work was £45,000 less than the Bank Manager's. Even today she would make a top class Project Manager."

The Ice Cream Parlour and ice cream van. Early 1990's.

"My Dad and Mum had always rented the old bungalow for ten shillings a week in the beginning. Much later the owner wanted to sell it and she offered it to Mum and Dad but they felt they were too old to buy. My sisters, Marie, Rita and I had a meeting but Rita didn't want to buy. In the end Marie and her husband, Jim, myself and Barbara signed an Agreement that the four of us would own it. After Dad died Mum coped alone for quite a few years. Mum had never learnt to drive so a neighbour of ours, Doreen Sopps had driven her on the rounds whilst Dad had remained at home selling ice cream from the stall. Another driver was Joan Page. Joan has worked for us for around thirty-six or thirty-eight years and she still does a bit of driving for us today."

Tony and Barbara Donnarumma on a 'Fun Day' special for the public at the Carlo's Ice Cream Parlour, West Wellow. Fifty-year anniversary celebration of Carlo's Ices in West Wellow from 1945-1995. Tony and Barbara's four grandchildren are on the left. Courtesy of Pat Sillence Archive, Lower Test Valley Archaeological Study Group (LTVAS), Romsey Town Hall.

"Mum also helped serving ice cream here for me on the odd lunch break when I was out with the van. With Barbara and myself living just two doors away at the ice cream parlour, we saw Mum each day or she would come to see us, and, of course, other people visited. Eventually Mum became too frail to be left alone so she went to live in a very nice care home in Romsey. We kept her old bungalow empty so that she felt she always had somewhere to come back to. My Mum's maiden name was Searles. It was a long time after she met my Dad that his Italian family accepted her. What can I say - a very hard worker; always behind my Dad, whatever he did; she was there for him. Just like my Grandmother Trofimena really; a very hard worker. Mum went out on the van whether she was fit or not. Mum was very religious, Church of England and went to church every Sunday; unlike my Dad, who was Roman Catholic but never really practised it. Mum died in October 1998 aged 85 years. A lovely character and everybody knew her."

Carlo and Thora Donnarumma outside their Ice Cream Stall, West Wellow, near Romsey. C.1985. Peter G Murrell.

CHAPTER 11
The Tea Rooms are Added and Anthony Carlo's Conclusions

"A customer came here one day and told me he had brought his family for ice cream but he himself didn't like it. He suggested that I ought to sell a cup of tea. I said 'I'll tell you what I'll do, I'll build a nice tea room for you!" The idea buzzed around in my head and I sat down to fathom out a suitable Planning Application which I described as 'Extension of existing accommodation for customers to sit and have ice cream'. However, after I got the Planning Permission I put up a sign for 'Tea Rooms'. The Planners tried to close me down so I told them 'Well, if you don't let me have the Tea Rooms sign, which everybody wants, then I'll just close the lot down'. I told them that we must go forward in this world. After a slight change of Application I succeeded and we opened the Tea Rooms in 1999."

Anthony Carlo and Barbara Donnarumma outside their Team Rooms, 2011.

"Barbara and I never had any money then because we'd spent it all on the building, so we had to do everything ourselves. I would get up at seven in the morning and boil the milk and make enough ice cream that I felt was adequate. I used to deliver to Romsey School and Hounsdown School at lunch times, so I'd have a girl come in here to serve whilst I went there and I'd take over when I got back. I had another lady who used to take the van out around Totton. We went into the school playgrounds and sold it to the children. We have done that since 1945. It's a nice idea. However, because of health issues for children now, we can no longer sell ice creams with chocolate flakes, nor crisps or sweets. We only sell ice cream at the schools."

"There was quite a lot to do, though everything was electric by then. The use of ice went out years ago. A lot depended on the weather. Over the years we've learnt to judge how much to make so we don't waste a great deal. We had no money to afford more than a few hours for staff, plus the fact that the business had to pick up because of the overheads."

Anthony Carlo Donnarumma, Ice Cream Manufacturer, Carlo's Ices, West Wellow. 1990's.

"Our daughter, Beverley, was running a catering business in Southampton. She would get up at five o'clock in the morning, make sandwiches and deliver them to offices and so on. She was pretty experienced in catering so I asked her if she'd like to pack up her business and come to work for her Dad, which she did. We then got busier and busier so I asked my wife's sister's son, Wayne Shaw, who was working at the Polygon Hotel, Southampton as a Catering Manager, if he'd like to come to work for his uncle. He said he would so I gave him the job. He's a very good organiser."

Wayne Shaw, Sadie Bevan and Manager, Beverley Davies. The full-time staff of Carlo's Ice Cream Parlour and Tea Rooms, 2011.

"Catering seems to be in our blood, although my son Anton (Anthony) doesn't have quite so much interest. He has a very good career marketing excellent golfing equipment. Anton and Sarah's son, Jamie, worked for us for a while. He's now travelling and working around Australia. Beverley and Russell's son, Christopher has trained as a Chef under Marcus Wareing. Christopher is now working at a five star spa hotel in the New Forest where he's a brilliant chef. Beverley and Russell's daughter, Nicola, is a hair-dresser and Anton and Sarah's daughter, Carley, works for a cruise travel agency."

Barbara and Tony Donnarumma with their children Beverley Davies and Anton (Anthony) Donnarumma. A family birthday party, at the Ice Cream Parlour, early 1990's.

"We are open seven days a week, fifty-two weeks of the year excepting Christmas Day and New Year's Day. For lunches we always cook roast beef every Sunday. Sometimes we roast pork and lamb as well. We have fresh potatoes and fresh vegetables, all cooked here on the premises. Nothing comes pre-packed. For afternoon teas the scones and cakes are made fresh every day. We get a lot of coaches bringing customers for cream teas though we also sell take-away cream teas. Right through December we do a Christmas menu - five or six courses with a complimentary glass of wine. We have seating for sixty and we join tables together for big parties."

"Throughout the week we serve a variety of lunches, sandwiches, baguettes, salads and snacks, with special menus for Mother's Day, Christmas lunches and other occasions. The Tea Rooms closes at four-thirty and the Ice Cream Parlour closes at six and in the winter at five. We used to open until seven."

Anthony Donnarumma, Linda Cadier (nee Wilde), Barbara Donnarumma, Brian Donnarumma (Nicolo's grandson), Stella Wilde (nee Donnarumma, Nicolo's daughter). Carlo's Ice Cream Parlour and Tea Rooms, December 2009.

"We now make ice cream in twenty-five flavours. I always make the basic flavours plus I alternate four other flavours each day. The ice cream is made fresh every day so I have to judge quantities, often depending on the weather. My ice cream contains no additives, preservatives or oil - unlike commercial ice creams which contain these or emulsifiers, stabilisers, milk powder or powdered eggs. My ice cream recipe is based on milk, butter, sugar and cream. Sizes and prices vary but we cater for both ends of the market. We can provide a £1 cone - I say that no child leaves here without an ice cream."

"We have a little section outside in the ice cream parlour garden where we keep rabbits, guinea pigs, a horse and chickens. Children love to see little animals walking about. We often have fluffy little chicks for them to admire."

"Our ice cream van does a round in Totton, the New Forest or Romsey areas every morning except Wednesdays. Everybody knows our van is arriving because of its chimes tune "The Bells of St. Mary's". We also visit Romsey, Halterworth and Testwood Schools and other schools in the area."

Wayne Shaw with Carlo's Super Ices van. 1990's.

"The Wellow Branch of Cancer Research raises around £3,500 each year from their various fundraising events held on our premises - Easter tombolas, Summer fetes, plants sales, dog shows, Christmas sleigh rides around our car park and the wheelie bin collection within our tea rooms."

Anthony Carlo Donnarumma with Diane Blackburn, Easter Tombola at Carlo's Ice Cream Parlour and Tea Rooms, 2007. Courtesy of Romsey and Wellow Group of Friends of Cancer Research UK.

"I wouldn't be where I am today without my wife, Barbara. She's been absolutely fantastic. She's also been a 'silver service' waitress at Goodwood House and other similar places. She's a brilliant Book-keeper, an imaginative house-keeper and a lovely wife. I couldn't have had anybody better and if I could marry her again tomorrow, I would. When we were young, everybody said it would never last - but it has."

Barbara Donnarumma, front row, third from left, with colleagues at Goodwood House. 1990's.

"Barbara has many hobbies including making porcelain dolls and their clothes as well as making furniture for dolls houses. She's made a doll of me as Carlo and also a miniature of me as a Bellboy with pill-box hat, red tunic, trousers and gloves. She made that as a Christmas present for me."

Bellboy doll hand-made by Barbara.

"We've been very fortunate. When our children, Beverley and Anton, were young we used to get in the car and head down to the south of France or places like that and rent a caravan. As our children got older they no longer wanted to come with us so we tried a little cruise and we fell in love with it and we're hooked on cruising now. The super-liners are not for us. We liked the old QE2 and ships like that where older people can relax."

Anthony Carlo and Barbara Donnarumma embark the Queen Elizabeth 2, 1995.

"We've cruised to many countries, though there are always other countries to see too. We've done about eighteen cruises on the QE2 and we always eat at Table 55 in the Queen's Grill. I'm a bit of a snob when we go away - we have a butler and canapés and wines - so we indulge ourselves. Well, I've worked hard all my life and so has Barbara. I started work on the sea and I still love the sea - except I'm one of the privileged passengers now. I'm looked after by the crew instead of myself as crew looking after the passengers. What a privilege!"

Anthony Carlo and Barbara Donnarumma at their favourite Table 55, Queens Grill, Queen Elizabeth 2, 1998.

"We've also been going to Florida now for twenty-three years to holiday and see friends. I once went to a wonderful restaurant there called 'The Colonnade' which was by a beach. In the window was a photograph and a sign which said 'This is us selling fish from a little tin shed - and this is us now". I said to Barbara 'I'm going to make Carlo's like that' - from my Dad's old ice cream hut to a really nice place - and we've achieved it. I've gone full-circle. I always say to my grandchildren 'Have a dream and make it come true' because whenever you dream you can make it come true - but you must want to do it. I still get up at seven o'clock each morning and go into Carlo's Ice Cream Parlour and Tea Rooms and I really enjoy what I do and the socialising with all of the customers. I say that the morning that I go to work and don't want to be there, that's the day I pack up - but I haven't had that feeling yet."

Anthony Carlo and Barbara Donnarumma embark The Queen Elizabeth 2 at New York.

Chapter 12
The Return to Minori 2011

At the beginning of June 2011, with Carlo's Ice Cream Parlour and Tea Rooms in the safe hands of their daughter, Beverley Davies and their nephew, Wayne Shaw, Tony and Barbara Donnarumma made a short pilgrimage to Minori. Their only other visit had been in 1983 when they had met up with Trofimena's nieces Maria Esposito and her sister, now deceased, and nephew Alphonse, now also deceased. On this return visit twenty-eight years later, Maria, now aged eighty-eight years, is the only close relative still living in Minori.

Together with my husband, Andrew, I planned to be in Minori at the same time though for us this was the first leg of our exploration of the adjoining province of Basilicata following in the footsteps of Carlo Levi author of "Christ Stopped at Eboli" 1935, and David Yeadon's recent book "A Year in Basilicata" 2004.

L to R Barbara Donnarumma, Tatiana (Maria's Carer), Rosa Apicella (grand-daughter of Maria), Maria Esposito (Trofimena's niece), Trofimena Apicella (daughter of Maria) and her husband, Ciro Apicella, Tony Donnarumma. Minori May 2011, at the home of Maria in Minori.

I was privileged to experience first-hand Tony's pride on this return to his family's roots. We toured the town, the cemetery and ancient historic remains. We visited Minori's official Registrar, Signore Antonio Pappalardo who was very helpful. We also visited the Basilica of St Trofimena though failed to meet up with the Priest, Don Pasquale Gentile who was busy.

Not only did we meet with Maria Esposito who is the niece of Tony's grandmother, Trofimena (nee Proto), we also met her daughter and son-in-law, Trofimena and Ciro Apicella. Maria's grand-daughter, Rosa Apicella had flown in from Milan to visit and was able to help with some translation. Maria remembered well her Aunt Trofimena. From around 1936 until her death in 1963 Trofimena had mostly lived in Minori. Trofimena Proto had been the sister to Immacolata and to Maria's mother, Carmella. The parents of the three sisters Trofimena, Carmella and Immacolata were Nicolo Proto and Maria Carmella Lamberti. Immacolata married Salvatore Di Lieto and emigrated to the USA where they had three children and never returned. Carmella married Signore Esposito, had five children but never left Minori. Trofimena married Achille Donnarumma, emigrated to England but returned alone.

Trofimena Donnarumma (Proto) in a photographic studio C.1926 Southampton. Courtesy of Elise Edwards (nee Donnarumma).

The economic environment of Minori today has vastly changed from the Minori left behind by Achille and Trofimena Donnarumma in 1905 just after their marriage. We know that Achille had been working in England, possibly as far back as 1894 when he was just fourteen years of age. However, he probably worked a return sea-passage to Minori where he met and married Trofimena Proto. The marriage entry states her profession to be a 'Domestico' and his to be that of a 'Mariner'. It is interesting to note that the births of their first six children, all born in Southampton, England, have been registered at the L'Ufficiale dello Stato Civile, Minori in 1915; their seventh child having not been born until December 1915. These registrations were most probably done by Achille when he returned to Italy to serve in the 1st World War.

View of Minori from jetty. May 2011.

In 1905 the main employers of this fishing village were the owners of the lemon orchards, the hand-made paper-making industry, flour mills, ceramics factory and the pasta-making factory. Indeed, with Achille's father's uncle, Reginaldo Donnarumma (born 1815) having been an 'Industrialist' in Minori, owning one or more of these business, the surname of Donnarumma would therefore have been fairly prominent. This is not least because a son of Reginaldo, called Carlo, born 1849, became the High Priest of the Basilica of St. Trofimena. Diocesian Canon Don Carlo Matteo Donnarumma died in 1922. Achille's father (Domenico) and grandfather (Nicolo) were also Church Organists at this Basilica which had once been a cathedral.

There are no descendants with the surname of Donnarumma living in Minori today although the name appears several times in the Salerno-Sorrento telephone directory. However, the name appears more often, especially in businesses, in the town of Gragnano, north east of Sorrento. Gragnano is world-famous for its specialist pastas. There are strangely no gravestones or memorials in the Minori cemetery bearing the name of Donnarumma, excepting that of the High Priest. Trofimena's remains are reputedly buried in the Proto family vault, though some members of the family believe they are within the Gennari Lamberti and Castellano family vault. Trofimena's mother, Maria Proto, was born Maria Lamberti.

Minori looking towards Ravello, above. May 2011.

Minori remains a small authentic southern Italian coastal village though without its major factories. Lemon orchards survive along with small family-run restaurants, trattoria and a few hotels. Fishing from small boats is also carried out. There are minor businesses making gelato (ice cream), the lemon liqueur called 'Limoncella', and pasta. The most typical are ndunderi, scialatielli and ricci (a type of fusilli). Attractive ceramics and tiles are also made. The small beach and jetty nestle beautifully between the rising hills and mountains. As part of the charming Amalfi Coast it attracts tourists though in much smaller numbers than its more famous busy neighbours, Ravello, Amalfi, Positano, Sorrento and the Isle of Capri. The paper-making and pasta-making factories have disappeared though on the outskirts of the town, Marmorata, one of the original paper-making factories is now a very beautiful hotel and tourist apartments.

Minori, looking towards Marmorata holiday apartments and the elegant Marmorata Hotel, both modernised today from the ancient hand-made paper factory.

The following photograph is a fitting conclusion to my voyage of discovery and the history of Achille Donnarumma and Trofimena Proto, the parents of Carlo Donnarumma, Anthony Carlo's father. Whilst this account has followed Carlo's line, I have expanded a little on the genealogy of his siblings and other family members which I relate beneath the Donnarumma Family Tree in the Appendices. There lie many more chronicles. However, this story concludes where it began, in Minori, Southern Italy.

Barbara and Anthony Donnarumma at Villa Rufolo, Ravello. Below is the town of Minori. May 2011.

The following is a poem taught by Trofimena Proto Donnarumma to her grandson, John Richardson (Goodie's son, born 1933) when he was living with her in Minori from around 1936-1939 before the 2nd World War. When John was returned to Southampton by his grandmother he spoke only Italian. Trofimena lived in the second from top apartment at 13, Via S.Giorgio Mare, on the West of Minori. The tall building is a converted ancient fort which is still there today. Trofimena's windows and balcony overlooked the sea.

Neapolitan Poem - The Sea "il Mare"

Sono bello, sono maroso
Alle volte sono brioso
Senza alberi, senza fiore
Alle volte grande il sfavore

"The Sea" can be translated as:

I am beautiful, I am tempestuous
At times I am lively or light-hearted
Without trees, without flowers
At times I can be very ferocious

Epilogue
In Images

Anthony Carlo and Barbara Donnarumma
Making Ice Cream Today, 2011.

Four Generations of Donnarumma Caterers with the Author

Carlo Donnarumma (Achille and Trofimena's son) with Christine, 1985.

Anthony Carlo Donnarumma (Carlo and Thora's son) with Christine, 2009.

Beverley Davies (nee Donnarumma, Anthony and Barbara's daughter) with Christine, 2011.

Christopher Davies (Beverley and Russell's son) with Christine, 2010.

Appendix I

Reginaldo Seniore Donnarumma
m.
Giuditta Palumbo

Domenico Ruocco, b 1772
m.
Agnes Cioffi, b 1774

Donnarumma Family Tree - Early Years

Domenico Donnarumma, b.1792
m. (1814)
Trofimena Ruocco, b.1797
d. 13.2.1894

Reginaldo Donnarumma, b.1815
m.
Margherita Landi

Reginaldo Donnarumma,
b 1815
Factory Owner/Industrialist

**Nicolo Donnarumma,
b. 1817
Church Organist**

Rachele Lucia Donnarumma,
b. 1819

Alfonso Donnarumma,
b. 1820

Maria Carmela Donnarumma
b. 1823

Chiara Donnarumma,
b. 1825

Maria Concetta Donnarumma,
b. 1831

Magantila Mariangela
Donnarumma, b. 1834

Elena Donnarumma,
b. 1837

Maria Carmela, b 1842
(m. Giuseppi d'Amato,
1865 and had 9 children)

Carlo Matteo Donnarumma
b. 16.1.1849–d. 24.1.1922
High Priest of Basilica St
Trofimena, Minori

*No details about other
children*

**The further family tree
on pages 120 and 121
continues the line of
Nicolo Donnarumma,
b 1817**

Appendix II

Nicolo Donnarumma b.1817
Church Organist, deceased by 1897
m. 1845
Marianna Fago

Domenico Donnarumma b.1848
Church Organist, died after 1910
m.1873
Mariantonia Clotilde Lembo

Rosalia,	b.1846
Domenico,	**b.1848**
Reginaldo,	b.1850
Gerardo,	b.1853
Alfonso,	b.1856
Lucia,	b.1859
Francesco	b.1862
In London, 1891 census	
Maria Teresa	b.1866

Nicolo, b.1877, *to London*
Carlo, b.1878, *to Southampton*
        d.24.11.1923
Achille, b.1.3.1880, *to Southampton*
        d.2.5.1939
Details of other children unknown

Donnarumma
Family Tree -
Later Years

Achille Donnarumma d.1939
m. 20.7.1905 in Minori
Trofimena Proto
b.11.3.1879, d.10.1.1963

Carlo Donnarumma
m.1930 d.1990
Thora Searles
d.1998

Anthony Donnarumma
m. 1959
Barbara Pound

Nicolo,	b.1906 d.1977
Carlo,	**b.1908 d.1990**
Domenic	b.1909 d.1986
Eleonora, (Yana)	b.1911 d.2005
Clotilda, (Goodie)	b.1912 d.1998
Amalia, (Emily)	b.1913 d.2004
Francesco, (Babe)	b.1915 d.2003
All born in Southampton, England	

Marie, b.1932
Rita, b.1935
Anthony, b.1938

Beverley, b.1962
Anthony (Anton)
b.1964

The Grandchildren of Achille & Trofimena.

Nicolo's children
Nicolo Joseph
Raymond
Stella
Mario
Grace

Carlo's children
Marie
Rita
Anthony Carlo

Yana's children
Tony Peden
Mena Peden
Eddie Peden
Michael Peden

Goodie's child
John Richardson

Emily's child
Bruce Salak

Francesco's children
Colin
Elise

Domenic had no children

BIBLIOGRAPHY

Allen, Tudor. (2008) "Little Italy - the Story of London's Italian Quarter". Camden Local Studies and Archives Centre.

Bellows, Jim. (2001) "My Southampton - in the 20's and 30's". ELSP publishers.

Bettina, Elizabeth. (2009) "It Happened in Italy - Untold Stories of How the People of Italy Defied the Horrors of the Holocaust". Thomas Nelson USA.

Brooks, Clive and Boyd-Smith, Peter. (1989) "A History of Southampton in Picture Postcards". Ensign Publications.

Broomfield, Padmini. (2008) "Twenty-Five Years of Southampton Voices". Unpublished Special Edition of Southampton Oral History Unit (SOHU) Newsletter. Southampton City Council.

Colpi, Terri. (1991) "The Italian Factor - The Italian Community in Great Britain". Mainstream Publishing.

Colpi, Terri. (1991) "A Visual History of the Italian Community in Great Britain". Mainstream Publishing.

Diamand, Dr Salim. (1987) "Dottore! - Internment in Italy 1940-1945". Mosaic Press, USA and London.

Ford, Percy. (1931) "Work and Wealth in a Modern Port - An Economic Survey of Southampton". George Allen and Unwin Ltd. Thesis D.Phil, University of London.

Gadd, Eric Wyeth. (1988) "Southampton Through this Century". Paul Cave Publications Ltd.

Gadd, Eric Wyeth. (1979) "Southampton in the Twenties". Paul Cave Publications Ltd.

Gallaher, Tony. (1995) "Southampton's Inns and Taverns". Poulner Publishing Ltd, Ringwood.

Gallaher, Tony. (2007) "A Century of Southampton - Events, People and Places over the 20th Century". Sutton Publishing.

Howard-Bailey, Chris. (1990) "Down the Burma Road - Work and Leisure for the Below-Deck Crew of the Queen Mary 1947-1967". Oral History Team, Southampton Local Studies Section.

Hodgson, Maie. (1992) "Child of the Ditches". Typeset and printed by Fleetwood Print, Southampton.

Jemima, Sheila (Ed.) (1991) "Chapel and Northam - An Oral History of Southampton's Dockland Communities 1900-1945". Oral History, Southampton City Council.

Legg, Penny. (2010) "Southampton Then and Now". The History Press.

Leonard, AGK. (1984) "Stories of Southampton Streets".
Paul Cave Publications Ltd.

Levi, Carlo. (1947) "Christ Stopped at Eboli". Farrar, Straus and Company. 1948
Penguin Books, 1982, 2000.

Marr, Commodore Geoffrey T. (1973) "The Queens and I". Adlard Coles Ltd.

Oral History Team, Southampton. (1989) "Woolston Before the Bridge". Sheila
Jemima, Christine Tanner, Donald Hyslop. Southampton Local Studies Section.

Puleo, Stephen. (2007) "The Boston Italians - A Story of Pride, Perseverance
and Paesani, from the Years of the Great Immigrations to the Present Day".
Beacon Press, Boston, USA.

Rance, Adrian B. (1980) "A Victorian Photographer in Southampton -
Thomas Hibberd James". Paul Cave Publications Ltd.

Rance, Adrian. (1986) "Southampton - An Illustrated History".
Milestone Publications.

Rance, Adrian. (1985) "Southampton Then and Now". Milestone Publications.

Sandell, Elsie M. (1953) "Southampton Cavalcade". G.F. Wilson & Co Ltd.
Southampton.

Sandell, Elsie M. (1958) "Southampton Panorama". G.F. Wilson & Co Ltd.
Southampton.

Sponza, Lucio. (1988) "Italian Immigrants in Nineteenth Century Britain:
Realities and Images". Leicester University Press.

Sponza, Lucio. (2000) "Divided Loyalties - Italians in Britain During the Second
World War". Peter Lang AG European Academic Publishers, Bern.

Santulli, Michele (2011) "Modelle E Modelli Ciociari nell'arte Europea a Roma,
Parigi e Londra 1800-1900". Isola del Liri, Grafiche Pisani.

Tanner, Christine P. (1993) "Coming to Terms with the Past -
The Life Review and Its Applications in Social Work and Probation Practice".
Unpublished MSc dissertation. Southampton University.

Wellow History Society. (1981 reprinted 2010) "Wellow That Were".
Lower Test Valley Archaeological Study Group. The Studio Printers.

Yeadon, David. (2004) "Seasons in Basilicata - A Year in a Southern Italian
Hill Village". Harper Collins Publishers.

www.ancestry.co.uk

www.findmypast.com